What Others Are Saying About a Path to Abundance ~ It's Your Time!

From the moment I met Daphne and listened to her, I knew she was the real deal. Reading her book, you'll see exactly what I mean. She is a woman of action—someone who got great clarity on her purpose and has moved forward without hesitation to manifest the exact life she wants. By putting this into book form, she has empowered you to do the same. Let her story be a catalyst for your own forward movement. Well done, Daphne!

Amy Stoehr, PCC, Executive Coach, McLean International and Founder and Director, Real Estate Masters Guild

Well done! Highly recommend this book. With passion and conviction, Daphne truly demonstrates "What you Believe, You can Achieve!"

Peggy McColl, New York Times Best-Selling Author

My experience with Daphne has been life changing. Deep down within my soul, I wanted to believe that I could succeed in business but wasn't sure how to go about it. With Daphne's help, it was easy for me to apply a new set of belief systems to my own circumstances and life. After a weekend of discussion and how to apply this new way of thinking, I was able to see how I could achieve the life of my dreams.

Daphne's excitement and her own journey to success have shown me that it is possible. She helped me see that I was no different than any successful business owner, and that if they could achieve financial freedom, I could too!

She has a passion for life that is contagious. Any time spent with her can only be of benefit to your life and your own personal success. I look forward to learning more and growing my business with the help of Daphne and her incredible vision. Her demeanour exudes integrity, pride and dignity. She is a gift.

Louise McDougall-Gudzowaty, "The Little Red Yoga Barn"

Without procrastination, courage will conquer fear . . . Daphne tells you the "how to" in this book. Dedication, commitment, perseverance, and a genuine love of helping others succeed, are just a few of her many qualities compassionately shared with you in this book. If this doesn't knock you off the fence you are sitting on, nothing will.

Stan Newman, Broker/Owner of RE/MAX professionals, Recipient of RE/MAX Western Canada's coveted Robert H. Cherot Award

Path to Abundance
It's Your Time

DAPHNE SHEPHERD

Published by
Hasmark Publishing

1-888-402-0027

All Scripture quotations are taken from King James Version of the Bible.

Editor, Sigrid Macdonald
sigridmac@rogers.com

Cover Design, Killer Covers
www.KillerCovers.Com

Layout, DocUmeant Designs
www.DocUmeantDesigns.Com

First Edition, 2015

ISBN-13: 978-1-988071-06-0
ISBN-10: 1988071062

Dedication

To Dennis, my husband, whose encouragement, guidance, love and inspiration are a part of every page in this book.

To my wonderful family and a special expression of deep love and gratitude to my mom and dad.

Contents

Foreword by Bob Proctor

*T*he yellow brick road. The pot of gold at the end of the rainbow. Ask the average person off the street to imagine a path to abundance, and I suspect these are some of the images that might come to mind. And though the images may be grand, as metaphors, they contain a fatal flaw.

Oh, there's abundance available to you, all right. Lots of it… an INFINITE amount. And, yes, there is a path that is guaranteed to take you to it. But you aren't separated from either one of those things from anything like an ocean, a road or any other external stretch of space or time.

The journey along the path to abundance isn't a movement forward, toward something "out there." It is a turning inward, toward something you already possess and have possessed since the day you made your debut on this planet. In fact, long before.

Daphne Shepherd has exemplified this truth in one of the most dramatic ways possible. The extraordinary physical transformation she underwent in her life would seem, to an outside observer, to be purely external.

But as she knows, and describes so beautifully in this book, the real transformation happened inside first and was completed there long before it ever manifested in her physical world. Daphne embarked on an internal path—a mental path, a path of thinking—that led her to a limitless inner reservoir of riches. Using her mental faculty of imagination, she sculpted not just the body she wanted . . . but the career she wanted . . . the wealth she wanted . . . the LIFE she wanted: shaped and perfected them inside the studio of her mind until they were so clear and vivid, they could not help but manifest in her physical world.

That, in and of itself, is a marvellous thing. But what she is doing by sharing this story, her path, puts her on a different plane entirely. I've spent over 50 years sharing this information with people. I believe in it to the core of my being. My own life is a testament to this truth every single day, just as Daphne's is. She describes a process in these pages that is going to change lives. Those changed lives are going to change their worlds . . . and ultimately, THE world.

Daphne has embedded a remarkable message in the title of this magnificent book: It's your time. She's right. IT IS. And do you know what? It always has been. All you have to do is decide to seize it, and everything will be different for you. You will be on your way . . . on your path to abundance.

Bob Proctor, Best-Selling Author of *You Were Born Rich*

Preface

*T*his book has found its way into your hands for a reason, not by coincidence or accidentally. It is a book of awakening and learning about a powerful connection that is available to all of us; however, most of us do not have this awareness. It is about the power of your thoughts. It is about tapping into an infinite Source that will radically change your life as you once knew it. This book is about activating your brilliance. It's also about reflecting on your deepest values and where they were derived. Is your current situation and what you are doing today serving you or eroding you?

This book is for those of you who are searching and want to "shift" because you feel an internal stir. This stir or feeling of displacement may be something you have been feeling for a very long time, or maybe you recognize it's time today to make that shift for future benefit. A shift so powerful that you will begin to establish and create new behaviours that will in turn initiate a positive chain of events. A transformation within you where you take charge and become the visionary of your very life. It is about learning about the law of attraction or law of vibration, as they are one and the same, and your role not only in your own life but also within our universe, of which we are an integral part. It is a book about celebration of Spirit—your Spirit!

The goal of my book is to outline fundamental principles that will introduce you to the way you can unlock the treasure chest which contains the secret to tapping into your highest potential so that you can achieve optimal living on your terms. Truth is, your endeavour to learn and understand about this and other laws that govern our universe is not a trendy, "New Age" phase. Rather, it has been an on-going subject of study for many great historians—present and past, scientists, theologians, quantum physicists and many more for centuries. There is an answer, a common denominator, and the exciting news is that it is right in front of you.

Learn about the confines of limiting beliefs so you can engage in actions that break you free from the retaining walls of the mind and deliver profound benefits to you. Open yourself to the possibilities that lie within these pages if you yearn to explore a new dimension of your life's canvas that can drive you to fuller expression, joyful awareness, beautiful energy and freedom from a place of your truest, most pure and best self. Step into the power you already possess to create and shape a magnificent life that will leave an indelible mark within the hearts of those you love and a lasting legacy for all to embrace—It's your time!

"Someday, you're going to wake up and there won't be any time left to do the things you've always wanted to do."
—*Paulo Coelho, author of* The Alchemist

Acknowledgements

A book, like all of creation, is a process that starts as a seed and reaches its intended purpose through a magnificent process orchestrated by Mother Nature. From planting through gestation, coupled with the hands of compassion and nurturing, to the cultivation and harvest, this project has endured that journey. I am incredibly humbled and grateful to the people who inspired and supported me and have had an everlasting and significant impact on my life. I am forever thankful and blessed for the opportunity to channel this information, so it can flow to others.

To my husband, Dennis Kiel, who deserves the most thanks and to whom I am forever humbly indebted as my partner in everything! Thank you so much for your tireless belief in me, for sharing with me your remarkable strengths and for being my ever-patient and loving rock of support. I love you eternally, and you are the very best partner the law of attraction could ever have brought to me!

To my parents, Ruth and Jim: you are the most amazing and wonderful people I could ever have asked to be my parents. You have given me unlimited and unconditional support and love and continue to be inspirational role models, best friends and my mom and dad. I love you!

To my mentor, Bob Proctor, and his awesome team at Proctor Gallagher Institute, with special thanks to Gina and Sandra Gallagher for your universal belief and powerful, relentless commitment in empowering and helping others achieve their true potential on their personal quests to lead phenomenal and most magnificent lives.

Thank you to my friend and associate Stan Newman, Broker/Owner of RE/MAX professionals, who recognized and believed in my talent. Stan saw in me what I didn't see in myself. In February 2015, Stan was the recipient of the RE/MAX of Western Canada's highest honour, the Robert H. Cherot Award for leadership, business acumen and contribution to change within the industry; a fitting testament to his character and unwavering devotion.

To Peggy McColl, who is the best-of-the-best and has a special gift. Thank you for all your enthusiasm, laughs and guidance during our one-on-one coaching sessions.

To my editor, Sigrid Macdonald: thank you for your remarkable talent, expertise, kindness and dedication to this project. You are truly caring, and your ability to bring about precision and clarity is unparalleled.

To Amy Stoehr, PCC Executive Coach, McLean International and Founder and Director, Real Estate Masters Guild: thank you for being incredible, beautiful and generous YOU! I feel a special connection, and you have been a source of sheer inspiration to me through your successes within the real estate industry, coaching and mentoring.

To our beautiful friends who are a source of inspiration and a great gift that we are so blessed to have shared in our lives. A special thanks to Dorothy and Mark, Mo and Louise; your light shines forever in our hearts.

To my wonderful friend, Catherine Schellenberg: thank you for our awesome friendship! You are truly a gift, and I thoroughly enjoy our real estate Friday networking sessions. I thank you for your encouragement, support and for all your wonderful professional, fun and light-hearted insights!

To Mark, Craig and Susanne: Thank you for being the world's greatest siblings! Though we are all nestled in our unique geographical locations, every time we are together, my heart floods with love and laughter and pens another page of "great and memorable times!" in my Book of Life.

A special thanks to my beautiful sister, Cynthia . . . I absolutely love and adore you! Your contribution in transcribing the text is greatly appreciated, and our collaboration on the "big idea" continues to inspire me. Your beautiful light will shine forever in my heart!

Only as high as I reach I can grow, only as far as I seek can I go, only as deep as I look can I see, only as much as I dream can I be.

—*Karen Ravn*

Introduction

*O*ne. A beautiful and simplistic word. We are one with each other, and we are one within this beautiful universe we are living in, with time that has been gifted to us. I have written this book with a deep respect and love for you, as we are one of the same. Doesn't matter your geographical location—whether you are in Kelowna, British Columbia; Las Vegas, Nevada; London, England; or in the Caribbean—we walk in unison. Doesn't matter the language you speak. Doesn't matter the colour of your skin or what age or gender you are. Doesn't matter your traditions, religion, profession or schooling. We are made up of the same, and we are all governed by the precise laws of the universe. Where we are different is in our level of awareness and in our results. Where we are different is in the certain ways we do things, perhaps because of our belief systems, or the environment we grew up in, or our behavioural patterning. Or maybe because of conditioning passed to us by others.

Our senses (sight, hearing, smell, taste and touch) are continuously picking up stimuli and ideas, like the statuesque lighthouse on the coast, scanning the vast ocean of motion that spans for miles in front. When a signal or stimuli is received through our senses, it filters into our conscious minds—our intellectual minds or our reasoning minds—where we have the ability to accept the thought or idea and using the faculty of our imagination, build an image, a picture that is then embedded on the screens of our subconscious minds, or we can simply reject it. Interestingly, a thought is a thing, a cosmic wave that permeates all space and time and has a frequency that sends an electrical impulse, a frequency and impulse that can be scientifically measured. These thoughts generate within us emotions that ultimately motivate the choices we make. The thought frequency we emit dances within the energy field that is our universe, universal (infinite) intelligence. We live in a very orderly universe that is energy, and what we ultimately sense through our material experiences is that energy brought into form through the law of physics, through our thoughts. We are energy, an extension of our Creator and as such, infinite intelligence, power and perfection also exists within you. To know this is the foundation to understanding the secret of life.

We are gifted a limited time on earth to co-create, to tap into the infinite supply of vitality and abundance that is rightfully ours and to serve the greater good. We are energy conduits in physical form, and we are spiritual beings. Spirit is everywhere: omnipresent throughout the whole of creation, in all places, at all times, and in all things that animate our every act. And it is through our thoughts that we ultimately create and shape our reality. What is currently in your life through physical expression has been created by you through the aggregate of your thoughts.

I know it may be confusing to navigate through these principles, but they are the core fundamentals. You will understand these concepts better as we will be revisiting them often throughout the pages ahead. Keep an open mind as you read, and take time to absorb the content and I encourage you to jot down any notes on how you feel as you read. I have provided an "Activating your Brilliance ~ Points to Ponder" section at the conclusion of each chapter to help prompt you in your creative thinking. I would also encourage you to listen closely to the voice of your intuitive internal whispers. There will be a treasure of clues for your own personal journey within these.

Let's explore the dynamics of our thoughts. If we choose to accept a thought and utilizing the gift of our imagination become emotionally involved and connected to it through our heart, where the purest clarity of our life purpose lies, it is then impressed upon our subconscious minds.

Remember that the first point of reference is in the conscious mind, which sifts and filters through the information received from our five senses where we choose to either embrace or eliminate the information. Now, let's look at our subconscious mind. If the thought from the information received through our senses is accepted and is in harmony with the desires or internal inclinations in our heart space, we are said to be in alignment and connected to our truth. So what does that feel like? We feel good; we feel fulfilled and inspired by our truth, through our core purpose, as the path to abundance, which is our birthright, is illuminated within. You beam with confidence, vitality and you radiate beauty while simultaneously walking on the red carpet of hope and faith. Start now to explore and believe these fundamental principles on every level of your consciousness. When you do you will no longer labour under the limitations caused by the pollution and noise from the outside world that distorts our awareness, the purity of who we are and our life purpose, and that which only broadcasts false impressions, which instill within us fear, worry and doubt. Understand that fear will derail you—fear will ensure you walk in concrete shoes and will fast track you to an inner chaotic state and intellectual drought. It is key that you get into the habit of confronting and dissecting your debilitating fears with the goal of ultimately eliminating them.

It goes without saying that we must listen carefully to our thoughts. David James Lees once said, "Be mindful of your self-talk. It's a conversation with the universe."

The conscious mind can accept or reject a thought. It is the objective part of your mind where you make all your decisions and can reason. The subconscious mind, however, does not. It will accept the habitual thinking bestowed from your conscious mind, no questions asked. Whether it is deemed reasonable or not, whether it is truthful or not. Your subconscious mind is the emotional sphere and is also where your creativity stems.

What we hold in the powerhouse of our subconscious minds is then expressed physically through our bodies, which function as instruments of the mind—much like a tuning fork synchronizes a vibration—in alignment with the thought. This is where the law of attraction or law of vibration enters in and these laws will be used interchangeably throughout the book (the first law being the law of vibration). When we feel good, we are said to be in a positive vibration, and the law of attraction dictates that like-energy attracts like-energy. If we are feeling bad, we are said to be in a negative state of vibration, which is our internal diagnostic signal that we are not living in accordance with our true self and can only attract negative energy. Our *feelings* are our conscious awareness of the vibrations we are in.

We have tremendous creative faculties within us as co-creators on this journey, and we have the ability to use our imaginations to project ideas, to solve deficiencies in our lives, and to sow the seeds of anything we desire and want to manifest in our lives. For what lies within the seed is everything necessary for deliberate creation. But many of us were not taught that or were dissuaded from properly using this very powerful tool. Tragically, we were discouraged from adopting this truism as children during our most impressionable years—a time when our imaginations were spilling over with the infinite possibilities and outrageous dreams that were ours for the taking; a time when our belief that we could do, be and have anything we desired was ironclad; a time when our eyes opened to the size of dinner plates from the sheer excitement of the thought of conquering our innermost, secretive dreams; a time when we were invincible and not bound by any limitations in our minds; a time when we would don our capes, leap from the living room couch announcing our presence for all to hear "Ta da!" Much of the time, this was stripped away when we were told to "settle down, not to be silly, to simmer down and pay attention." Well, that's right. You guessed it. Over a period of time, a cumulative total of many years, this repetitive message severed the lifeline to our imaginative and creative thought potential.

> Imagination is everything. It is the preview
> of life's coming attractions. —*Albert Einstein*

Well, it's your time to upset the apple cart and reconnect with your truth, your co-creative self, for within the heart lies clarity of your life's purpose. Today, you are at a pivotal point. Keep focused and riveted to the song of your inner chorus and play the music that you came here to play. Begin to plant the seeds of your most fanciful dreams and desires! I'm speaking of those dreams that even appear delusional at present. We can be sure we are on the right path when our dreams, our goals, are of such magnitude that they create an emotional stir and "scare" us. Think and dream big from this heightened level of conscious awareness, and believe there is *magnificence* within you just waiting for your endorsement. As you journey, strive to move away from the attachment to the outcome and live in the meaning instead. Now that we've spent some time on the fundamentals, there is one more element we need to discuss. Desire. Desire or our internal inclinations are the catalyst to unlocking the unique combination to your highest potential and will be different for each of us.

From the mindset of gratitude, good health, spiritual prosperity and material wealth, become a curious student with the desire to evolve and grow. Then go forward from the place of already being in possession of these characteristics with an unwavering faith and put the information to work.

Sow the seeds, and give rise to the essence of who you are, for how can you harvest an abundant crop without planting the seeds? I am speaking of the ability to think on a higher plane of conscious awareness filtered through your intellectual faculties, coupled with the knowledge and understanding of the universal laws by which we are all governed. Do you know that thinking is the highest function human beings are capable of? All the great leaders have been in complete and unanimous agreement on one thing and that is, you become what you think about most of the time.

> "For as [a man] thinketh in his heart, so is he" *(Proverbs 23:7).*

I have been studying and applying these laws now since 2007 after watching the movie, *The Secret,* and my life has changed phenomenally. I knew I had to make a complete break from my path in life and re-ignite the passion I knew existed somewhere inside. I have written this book to share my humble examples and experiences with you and to encourage you to begin your journey of studying yourself and the very laws of *your being.* I live in a very small town, I had no formal education beyond grade 12 and am located one hour outside the closest city centre, yet, by studying, building a greater level of awareness, and committing to the process of abiding by these principles, I live a very fulfilled, prosperous and happy life. If you are currently experiencing disharmony in any aspect of your life, they are your personalized distress call, your "helloooo?" urging you to embrace quiet time for inner contemplation and indicating that it is time for a reset.

Essentially, we are fully alive when we are truly comfortable frequently dismantling our current reality with discretion and simultaneously allowing ourselves an openness to receive new thought-provoking information that will nurture our journey and take us to the next level in indulgence of fuller expression, enlightened understanding and heightened awareness. I'm thrilled and honoured that we've connected and that I get to share this journey with you. You are a magnificent being, and your stream of abundance awaits. It's your time!

Namasté,

Daphne

Namasté
(nah-mas-tay)

My soul honours your soul.

I honour the place in you where

The entire universe resides.

I honour the light, love, truth,

Beauty & peace within you,

Because it is also within me.

In sharing these things,

We are united, we are the same, we are one.

Activating your Brilliance—Points to Ponder

1) What is currently in your life through physical expression that you have created through the aggregate of your thoughts? These can be negative or positive. Schedule a ½ hour of quiet time with no distractions and journal them. Divide the sheet into two columns: Negatives in the left hand column and Positives in the right hand column.

2) If we accept the thought from the information we receive through our senses and it is in harmony with our desires, which reside in our heart space, we are said to be in alignment and connected to our truth. Place a *happy face* beside the top 3 positive points you have written that truly resonate in your heart space.

3) Our feelings are our conscious awareness of the vibration we are in. In general, what have you been feeling like? How do you feel about your top 3 positive and negatives?

Chapter One

The End Is Inevitable

*I*t is a fact that the mortality rate on planet earth is 100%. As sure as we all entered and exist in this wonderful and mysterious world of ours, the day we depart is inevitable.

This life process or journey we are all a part of is nothing short of miraculous! Each of us—with our genetic uniqueness, relations, geographical locations and individual experiences—travel along different paths that shape our existence, that shape our personalities and carve out our characteristics on our quest to live the good life defined on our terms.

We have all heard the adage that life is short, but what does that really mean? Let's stop and think about that for a moment. It will certainly have different meanings for different people. For example, if you or someone you know has lost a child, then those three words painfully resonate on a very deep and personal level that most people cannot relate to. Perhaps someone has been taken away tragically, or maybe someone who was just budding into beautiful form, at a prime time in their life, was labelled with a crippling diagnosis.

The lesson and "shout out" is, life is precious. None of us knows when it is our time. We don't know when we will take our final breath. We don't know when the diagnosis will come or how an accident will impair us. Nor can we look into a crystal ball and see this for others. What we do know is that in this very moment, we have today, and today is a magnificent gift. A gift of life and eternal love.

Why is it that we wait to do or experience the things we know we want in our lives? We wait or procrastinate in an irrational, self-sabotaging way, preventing us from living our lives in alignment with our core purpose and our truth. I've often heard people say, "I wish I would have." These have to be the saddest five words I've ever heard. Don't EVER catch yourself saying these words, for if you do, it's too late and I can't think of a greater tragedy than that. This waiting, wishing, procrastinating, results only in stolen moments. Don't wait for a diagnosis as a permission slip to go out and live the intentional and creative life you were meant to live. Unleash your inner child now, and follow your heart!

So what happens when we are so caught up in our hurried, mostly chaotic lives, rarely coming up for a breath? Trouble! We begin to lose perspective—perspective of time. Our bodies' change, and mental clarity diminishes as the ill effects of stress bind us. We hover in a state of numbness. We are essentially going against the grain—against the very natural laws of our being in our time-space existence.

So, let's first begin to gain an understanding of who we really are. We are living organisms made of molecular structure living in an orderly, ever-present and evolving universe governed by precise laws.

We are the extension of our Creator; we are conduits of Source Energy anointed and unified as one in physical bodies. Source Energy is omnipresent, and everything you see is an expression of this power. We live together, and we emit a vibration that is being responded to within the universe through the law of attraction. We have been gifted with deep reservoirs of infinite potential, creative and intellectual faculties and have full-rights access to an energy stream of endless possibilities. Every one of us. Our conscious and subconscious minds are like generators capable of thought, and with thought comes the ability to perceive. Along with perception comes the platform that enables us to draw contrast.

From contrast, we have the ability to make choices with the conscious awareness that infinite potential and creative power flows to and through us. We are beacons interwoven and unified with all of existence in this orderly and harmonious universe. You are light energy, a beautiful spiritual being, and it's your time to shine!

Our lives have profound meaning to our cherished friends, beloved family, associates, communities and co-workers. But also, our lives are precious within the vast universe, though we don't think of this on such a grand scale. We find it hard to imagine because of our lack of self-awareness and our self-limiting capacity to believe in the *big picture*. But we do make an integral impact on the universe. It is our responsibility, therefore, to embrace our life gift and to recognize the gift in others. To live and encourage others to live a fulfilling, engaged life of purpose that illuminates our Spirits; to light up and cast our rays onto others, so they, too, can feel the warmth, beauty and abundance life has to offer. Your purpose will always be found in service. Ask yourself, "How may I serve?"

I am not sure where this book finds you in your life, but with that inevitable deadline looming, now is not too soon to reset your purpose, take inventory of what is working for you and what is not, and then sculpt a renewed meaning and inscribe a new life script for a fulfilled, well-lived, purposeful life, lavish and spilling over into meaningful relationships, a blazing passion for the work you love, spiritual wealth, optimal health, financial abundance, and a legacy that continues to shine on long after your departure from this wonderful but short life. It's your time to create, to expand your palate and delight in the fruits of your intentional reality, to attract the good you desire, to live a profound and meaningful life. Just take this first small step with me in shifting your awareness. The greatest stumbling block toward progress in any endeavour is a closed mind. Open your mind to receive this information and, in reflection of your current life, give it wholehearted consideration. You'll be glad you did, and the truth is, you don't have to sit back and take whatever life throws at you. You have a choice.

Faith is taking the first step even when you don't see the whole staircase.
—*Martin Luther King, Jr.*

Say it with me—even if you don't believe it in this moment—"It's my time." In a quiet place, on the screen of your mind, post a current and relevant collage of pictures of your life. Acknowledge for a moment that this is where you are today and where your journey begins. Now, set aside those images and on the screen of your magnificent mind, broadcast a collage of pictures of the life you desire, pause and take note of the fragrance in the air, the simultaneous cadence of the distant hum of life playing in the background, the visual textures of your life canvas. Grasp those images by the lapels, lean in and say with me, "It's my time."

"Whatever you can do, or dream you can do, begin it. Boldness has genius, power and magic in it. Begin it now."
—*Johann Wolfgang von Goethe*

It is at this junction that a lot of people merely discard and dismiss this process as "wishful thinking." Why? Because at some point in their lives, they had a fleeting wish to own a red Lamborghini or win the mega lottery, and it failed to show up in their driveway or bank account the next day. In all probability, we've all experienced these thoughts, and this is where the rubber meets the road. It is by design that we have no idea how we are going to manifest our goals rooted from our desires. Though this may appear irrational and almost preposterous at this time, you will gain an understanding of this by the end of *Path to Abundance ~ It's Your Time.*

This journey is about authenticating you with your life purpose. So many individuals co-exist with a distorted, superficial sense of personality, a personality manipulated by ego, which breeds fear-based behaviours such as greed, arrogance, self-destructiveness, self-judgment and impatience. Ego imparts a set of different beliefs about who we are. This ego of ours says who I am, is what I have accomplished in life. It says who I am, is what I have and what I own. From this perspective, ego is also saying I am separate from everyone else. This breeds competition and as such fear based behaviours evolve. Isn't it time we, as a populace who are growing more agitated in a world that doesn't work, reconnect to our deepest core for the ultimate truth? Imagine for a moment if, as a global community we were all to light up just a little, how we could eliminate the dark. The dark within ourselves and the dark within others, egos checked aside. We need to move into a space without ego to connect with our spiritual essence.

Spirit is always about expansion and fuller expression and awaits our permission to provide us with the necessary resources required to germinate and fulfill our desires. As individuals on a physical plane, it is not about what we get but rather **who we become** on our journey. The image we have cast can only manifest in our physical world in one way, and that is through the precise laws of the universe and faith. Yes, faith. The faith I speak of is not wishy-washy faith but faith based on understanding. That is, faith interwoven on a heightened level of understanding from the highest self within us. Clarence Smithison once said, "Faith is the ability to see the invisible and believe in the incredible, and that is what enables believers to receive what the masses think is impossible."

When we are aligned and in harmony with our core truth and purpose, the resources will appear and pave your way to the means of achieving and manifesting your goals and desires. And, so it is then that Spirit must regard our desires and goals as worthwhile intentions that contribute to our overall path in life and serve the greater good.

We must let go of the life we have planned, so as to accept the one that is waiting for us.
—Joseph Campbell

Activating your Brilliance—Points to Ponder

1) Each of us—with our genetic uniqueness, relations, geographical locations and individual experiences—travel along different paths that shape our existence and personalities, and carve out our characteristics on our quest to live the good life defined in our terms. Journal the attributes of your genetic uniqueness, your relations with others and the experiences you have endured.

2) We wait or procrastinate in an irrational, self-sabotaging way, preventing us from living our lives in alignment with our purpose and in a way that resonates with our truth.

3) We have been gifted with deep reservoirs of infinite potential, creative faculties and have full-rights access to an energy stream of endless possibilities. Access these gifts through the gateway of your purest intentions. Affirm to yourself that you ARE abundance and that you ARE joy and light in perfect manifestation.

~◉ *Chapter Two* ◉~

Flight Path: The Altitude vs. Attitude Parallel

What Plane Are You Flying On?

The alarm pierces the air. It's 2:00 am on Friday, February 21, 2014, and I'm on my way to a seminar in Los Angeles. Excited, and with my heart racing from the abrupt awakening, I fumble my way to the bedroom window to look outside. Always a nervous flyer, the weather is my first consideration and thought of the day. I brush the drapes aside. CRAP! It's cloudy and cold, with brutal wind-chills. Next, I turn on the Weather Channel to see if the clouds are going to dissipate before my flight. I put the coffee on and hear, "cloudy with snow flurries all day—with no chance of sun." I'm devastated. Something about being stuck in an oversized toothpaste tube—that flies in atmospheric pressures we cannot breathe in—just doesn't sit well with me. Well, time to put my big girl panties on, finish packing and head to the airport.

From the time I leave the house, all the way to the airport, I mumble, "Really? Why me? What a crappy day. How could this be?" Even at the airport, it is clear that people are tired, and I can tell the ones who have slept in by their flattened-hairdo and dishevelled appearance. As I look around, I chalk it up to everyone feeling the effects of the cloudy, cold and snowy day ahead.

The early morning flight attendants are wide-eyed, professionally adorned and on when they welcome everyone aboard. As we begin to taxi, I look over the wings for loose screws, divots in the metal, oil or antifreeze leaks, and to make sure those pontoon-like structures mounted under the wings are in good condition. This is my personal, pre-flight observation ritual.

Next, the announcements come. "Welcome on board Flight 395 to Calgary, with service to Los Angeles. Our aircraft is under the command of our wonderful Captain with First Officer. Our flying time will be approximately 1 ½ hours, and we will reach a maximum cruising altitude of 32,000 feet. In preparation for take-off, please ensure that your seat backs and tray tables are in their full upright and stowed positions, your seatbelts are securely fastened and all your carry-on items are securely stowed. Thank you for your attention. We will be on our way and airborne shortly."

Our taxi continues, and I notice light, nervous chatter and darting eyes throughout the aircraft. The plane then comes to a complete stop. I know what's next, and I feel the terror flow through my veins. My palms are sweaty, and I recognize that

I'm experiencing the physiological phenomenon of the fight or flight response.

The powerful turbine engines begin to ramp up as we accelerate, and with our speed steadily increasing, we're gently compressed into our seats. There are a few bumps along the way that bounce the wings up and down, that make our plane look like an albatross attempting to fly. The wheels come up with a thump, and moments later wisps of white cloud pass by my little oval window. My grip relaxes a little, and I take a deep breath. Within the next few moments, fear strikes again. I can't see anything! It's like swimming in murky water and trying to see the bottom. The sheer terror stings through my every fibre. "What a crappy day," I catch myself thinking again.

The plane gets tossed about, and I grip the armrest thinking the worst, "We're all going to die." I'm desperately trying to see the wings to make sure they are both still attached. More bumps and dips, and now I'm seriously wondering about the integrity of the structure. It's taken a lot of cloud hits and inhaled a lot of cloud fluff, and most likely has felt the strain of having to correct itself from the unforeseen air pockets and turbulence that it has endured. I sit and wonder if we have deviated off course and I am painfully aware that if I can't see, then the Captain and First Officer also can't see.

Then all of a sudden, like a welder's flash, the sun appears. It is bright and intense, and the sky is clear and blue. The pitch of the engines changes, and we are well above the clouds, and have survived the turbulent time.

With a deep sigh and the warmth of the nurturing sun on my cheek, a sense of calm and well-being floods my veins. At that moment, I thought this experience was a great two-pronged analogy for life.

You know, isn't that the way life is sometimes? During our time on planet earth, we will all experience these cloudy, grey, brutally cold, daunting and chilling days. At times, these cloudy days will string one into the next, a successive pattern of despair with no promise of a break. Some last through a single incident, some a month, some cloudy with no end in sight. Some so turbulent and relentless that they uproot and destroy life as we once knew it on an emotional, spiritual and physical level.

So, how is it that we get through these treacherous times? First, understand that none of us are here alone though at the time of crisis, no matter what level, we feel isolation. Then the question: Why is this happening to me? At this juncture, it is key that we embrace Source and trust that an inkling of comfort shall come to us that will allow the opportunity to grasp the first thread of strength necessary to move toward healing. Then, it is a building upon this first thread and an endeavour to summon the necessary strength to step outside the circumstance, to step outside your current reality, and know that it just is. This is the ebb and flow of life, and we will all walk this path. It is during these times that we must reach out to the support structure of friends and family. It is also critical that we let go and trust. Our support structures are there to embrace and to provide a safe and trusted plat-form as we journey through the challenging times. They will breathe with us when we feel we are suffocating; the painful compression of experience reminiscent of an assault on our physical and emotional being. They are there. Source is also there, omnipresent and always walking with you and living within to see us through the turbulence until it breaks into the mystery of a renewed direction. A re-awakening of purpose without an immediate explanation. Trust that it will birth new meaning, as sure as the sun will rise tomorrow and the challenge of the turbulent time has poked and encouraged us to grow in new ways. It is time for deep reflection.

The second part of this analogy is what is experienced when we are carboned up and paralyzed by fear. Without doubt, as we embark upon our unique journey to discover our authentic self and extract our truth, we are going to experience ups and downs. This is part of growth. We are habitual beings, and it is our nature as human beings to coast on the path of least resistance. But beware, this stifles growth. This is where most of us are "comfortable" and yes, feel pretty good. However, when we think of expanding and taking a big leap of faith absent of a heightened understanding of how our universe operates, we entertain the possibilities but more often than not, we will say, "Who am I to take this on?" or "I can't do this because X is not present in my life." Or "I'm not good enough" or "It won't work" or "I'm not smart enough" or "What will my friends think?" and so on. In Chapter 6, I explain how fear powered down my quest to become a provincial bodybuilder. How it paralyzed me, which resulted in my request to decline from the competition.

Bob Riggs makes sense of this static holding pattern and articulates the identity of our safe place very well in his writing *The Comfort Zone.*

"Many of us have established a comfort zone in our lives. We're just coasting along taking the path of least resistance, and just getting by.

This is a very common and understandable attitude. We've all worked hard to get where we are, and it may seem a good place to be.

The problem with this is that once we stop reaching, stretching, seeking and risking, we actually stop growing. The comfort zone frame of mind is settling for what we are TODAY.

That may be fine today, but without continued growth, WE ARE NOW ALL WE ARE EVER GOING TO BE.

If you are in a comfort zone, beware ~ the danger of a comfort zone is that it doesn't hurt, and it may even feel good."

When we are coasting along and feeling good, understand that staying there would involve stagnation. Identify that this is your green light to stretch, to listen, tune in and feel the pull of life's next challenge leading you closer to the on-going fulfillment of your desires and purposeful existence.

And so it is; we know we want it, yet when we start to think of the logistics or what change it might mean to our current reality to possess it, and along the way we experience a few lumps and bumps, we bail. Just like the airplane departing from its familiar environment and coming into contact with it's *perceived ceiling* of clouds unaware of the calm and brilliance on the other side. If the airplane plays it safe and flies below the clouds, not only is it in danger of coming into contact with additional obstacles, it completely misses the beauty of the horizon! If the plane endures the turbulence, which it is built for, within a short period, it breaks through the clouds and flies effortlessly through a spectacular horizon. A completely different viewpoint. I encourage you to stop flying below the clouds; the view is nothing compared to the sensational, pristine view seen above the clouds. We are not gifted life to "fly low" but rather to be expressive and fabulous from the path of who we are.

Right now, take an all-present life breath, fasten your seatbelt and face the uncertainty—face the fear straight on. Start exploring the cause of your fear. If it is uncertainty, acknowledge that is just lack of awareness or lack of knowledge. Think back to your life purpose, your intention as co-creator on this planet, and ask if this fear-based emotion is serving you. You will discover quickly that it is a hindrance and threat to your unfolding. Refuse it. Wrestle it armed with positive thought, and embrace freedom from it. Make that choice. Choose your thoughts and remember. . . . they are a conversation with the universe and ultimately with yourself! It's your time!

"Obstacles are those frightful things you see when you take your eyes off your goal"
—*Henry Ford*

Activating your Brilliance—Points to Ponder

1) It is key that we embrace Source and trust that an inkling of comfort shall come that will allow us the opportunity to grasp the first thread of strength necessary to move toward healing.

2) Open your mind and your heart to a re-awakening of purpose that may be without an immediate explanation.

3) We are not gifted life to "fly low" but rather to be expressive and fabulous from the path of who we really are.

~ᵍ *Chapter Three* ᵍ~

Change the Meaning, Change Your Life!

"Nothing is impossible; the word itself says, 'I'm possible!'" —*Audrey Hepburn*

---

*E*very time you experience stress, you have a physiological and psychological reaction to it. This will always be, for all of us, for all time. Here's the bad news: from the physiological standpoint, stress is cumulative. What does this mean? That the ongoing experiences of stress in our life is built upon the previous one. That's right, we don't get the privilege of starting back at point zero. So if you are someone *who carries the weight of the world on your shoulders,* then this chapter will be life changing for you.

The Holmes and Rahe Stress Scale lists the top five life-altering stressors as:

1) Death of a spouse

2) Divorce

3) Marital separation

4) Imprisonment

5) Death of close family members

These will be the worst and most turbulent times that we will encounter. Some of us may not have experienced any of these yet. For others, once has already been painfully too much. As we journey, some of us parallel to one another, and some where our paths will cross. We will all lose someone dear to us or encounter a situation that will crush or deflate us. How do we begin to fathom moving on? How will it alter our core perception of this so-called wonderful world? How do we trust? How do we survive? For it is times like these, a very part of us also dies. We don't carry on—rather, we cope.

That is the sting we will experience in life. We feel a significant loss no matter the situation and mourn for what we believe could have been. The promise of and the possibilities swindled from us. These should never have been taken from us but the reality is otherwise.

We understand that as spiritual beings, an extension of Source Energy living in physical bodies, it is our responsibility to harmonize a life of expression with a life of purpose. This is accomplished when we realize our highest purpose, which then leads us to the realization of a life of fullest expression. It boils down to, know thyself.

Because, when we further study and embrace this concept, we can begin to change our perception of the meanings placed before us. It will help diminish the inevitable sting. Whether it is loss of a loved one, a marriage, a job, freedom, or loss of physical capacity, we have to decide how we will work through it. Without these necessary and comparative experiences, we would not be able to perceive any kind of understanding of the essence of who we are, within ourselves. The process, the sting from a life experience, is a necessary journey we will all endure.

When I was growing up, a funeral was a very sad, solemn day, where I had to come to terms that I would never see this person again. It was so final. So unfair. This emotion was based from previous observations of how most people responded at a funeral gathering. It wasn't until my 30s, when I attended a funeral where the minister opened by saying that we were gathered to "celebrate a fulfilled and well-lived life." *Celebrate?!* Well, throughout that service, we were prompted to think how fortunate we were to have had this person in our lives and to rejoice; to express gratitude for all the lessons we learned from them, for all the happy and memorable times we shared, for the examples they set for us that would continue to enrich our lives. They were a gift, and those of us left behind were fortunate to be intended receivers of their precious gift. There were moments of laughter and lively exchanges of conversation in remembering times past and honouring their Spirit. The important point to remember is that it is *your* journey, and you choose the path of interpretation that resonates with your truth and understanding. You choose your own thoughts. No one else can tamper with this truth.

Listen with respect to your inner conversation. This is a process that will take time. Stay focused on seeking new meaning of the life event and ask Source Energy to bring clarity, love and understanding to your state of being, whether a chaotic life event or simply in an inquisitive state. Be kind to yourself in this pursuit and find comfort knowing that each of us will cope a different way. We are all challenged intermittently with discouragement tests as life is not always fair. The *Life Manual* study guide in a downloadable PDF file doesn't exist, and this is where you begin to write the most important story ...your life story, which is written through the choices you make and experiences you have endured. Make the choice to seek new meaning when faced with a challenge. Walk in faith, and believe the crisis or upset can be transcended to result in a specific, alternative, meaningful purpose. The birth of a new perspective on life lies just ahead, and it is an opportunity for us to find deeper meaning within our lives. It stops us dead in our tracks and prompts us to examine and appreciate what matters; to look around in awareness through our "gratitude" glasses. It draws the contrast to be grateful for all our surrounding wonders, big or small, and reminds us not to take them for granted. To appreciate and to live fully; fully present in every moment gifted to you.

Several years ago, I held an administrative job in a company I loved. I had been there for quite some time, and thoroughly loved the job and the people I worked with. The company made a sudden shift in direction, and some of us were let go without warning. At day's end, the company provided us with a cardboard box to put our belongings in. My nervous system shuddered. I was in disbelief, and the old fight or flight stress response set in—from dry mouth to weak and shaking legs.

I remained unemployed and emotionally incapacitated for an entire year! I became angry, resentful and bitter.

Following that directionless year, I discovered a new passion: real estate. At the time, it was very scary—and a huge gamble—as I had never held a sales position before. I established a simple set of principles, and I worked very hard at branding myself and gaining experience and quickly became a well-respected name in the industry. But even with my newfound success, I was still deeply indignant about my treatment from the previous employer. My dismissal, and the way it was handled was, in my opinion, unjust and callous.

One day, while speaking to a friend, he said there were three steps for me to follow to resolve and release the toxicity from my system, and they were:

1) Accept what is (Bad things can happen to good people).

2) Harvest the good.

3) Dismiss and lock out the rest because it no longer serves.

It has no purpose in my life.

As I drove home, I contemplated our conversation. I certainly accepted the occurrence and acknowledged it *as is*. But it was the next step that was most profound for me; *harvesting the good*. I immediately thought, "What was good about taking a year of my life?" But, as I sat and thought, it was as though a shower of blessings rained upon me!

'Really? What *wasn't* good about it?' was my next question to myself.

1) I now worked with people I thoroughly enjoyed, making new friends.

2) I gained great experience and grew intellectually.

3) This job was a catalyst to my current position and business success.

4) I got into the best shape of my life!

5) It provided me the necessary canvas of contrast that enabled me to appreciate and express daily gratitude for all the magnificence of my life.

I wouldn't be where I am today had I not had that experience. That's how profound an impact it has had on me. It has furnished me a sensational lifestyle that keeps getting better and for which I am grateful every day.

The residual toxicity was no longer serving me, so I eliminated it. When I was able to harvest the good, then and only then, I was able to bleed the toxicity that had accumulated within. This experience challenged and presented me with contrast, which allowed for my expansion. The act of dwelling on it gave it a persona, which tainted my life experiences and bred the toxicity. Denying it meant I was acknowledging its existence, which is why acceptance of "what is, is" is the first step. So, instead of resisting, I was able to forgive in the light of appreciation for my expansion that was made possible through the experience. I improved and accepted its value (the experience); this melted the vile grip it once held, and I began to transcend from that place. These are our lessons in life, and the feeling of forgiveness and harvesting of good will always feel better than the feeling of laying blame. Change the meaning. Change your life. It's your time.

Activating your Brilliance—Points to Ponder:

1) Without these necessary and comparative experiences in our lives, we would not be able to perceive any understanding of the essence of who we are, within ourselves.

2) The *Life Manual Study Guide* in a downloadable PDF file doesn't exist and this is where you begin to write the most important story ...your life story, which is written through the choices you make and the experiences you endure.

3) Accept that what is, is (Bad things can happen to good people). Harvest the good. Dismiss and lock out the rest because it no longer serves. It has no purpose in your life. Write out a situation you have been struggling with and journal through the 3 steps.

Chapter Four

Your Defining Truth Premieres Today!

"Every day is a gift, and the point of power is in this moment." —*Daphne Shepherd*

---

*A*ccept that what was yesterday was. Yesterday has passed never to be repeated. Moving forward into today, we need to understand that we cannot let any of the negative events of yesterday, last week, last month or last year leech into the gift of our new day ~ today. It's about choice, your choice. Give thanks for the lessons learned yesterday. This is the way you disarm and free yourself from the drudgery of carrying the negativity that is of no service to your overall well-being. Think about that for a moment. On the flip side, you want to nurture and build upon the positive events you've experienced. Conjure that positive momentum to cast you forward wrapped in the emotion of feeling good, of feeling inspired and let these emotions liberate and free you. Because what does the law of attraction decree? Like attracts like. Think good and good will follow. Draw the line in the sand today, it's your choice and never say "I can't." Yesterday does not define who you are capable of becoming today. It's your time.

This chapter humbly encompasses the first of four personal examples I have incorporated in this book of how events, personal experiences, spiritual wealth and financial abundance have come to manifest in my life by following the principles of the law of vibration, tuning into a higher level of awareness and consciously creating my deliberate reality. Some of the names have been changed for privacy. This first story is about the defining moment when I turned inward, listened to the inner toxic conversation and then etched the line in the sand by making a choice that changed my world.

It all started with the Body-for-Life Challenge program and my quest to overcome the stumbling blocks that I fought tirelessly both emotionally and physically. Simply put, from a desire of wanting to feel and look better, I made a choice and cast an image on the screen of my conscious mind and got emotionally involved. My mind-set was one of deliberate creation and I ingrained the thought of already being a Top Finisher shortly after reading the book. I was so emotionally connected to this image that I could smell the cowhide leather and feel the weight of the prized "Champions" jacket on my shoulders as part of the prize package being offered. On a subconscious level, I repeatedly lived this scenario in my mind by focusing on the image, the mini-movie and feeling the moment of sheer exhilaration seeing author and Body-for-Life creator Bill Philip's limo pulling into my driveway to personally present me as a Top Finisher in the challenge in my age category. This was not an event that was going to *happen* to me; I was already in receipt of it, coming *from* the place of already having it in my subconsious mind. Not one doubt. Here's an interesting thing for you to know and was a key to my success in the program. Your subconscious mind cannot tell the difference between you having something in your possession or not having it. In Joseph Murphy's book "The Power of Your Subconscious Mind," he points out the following:

"Your subconscious mind accepts what is impressed upon it or what you consciously believe." He also points out: "Remember, your subconscious mind does not engage in proving whether your thoughts are good or bad, true or false, but it responds according to the nature of your thoughts or suggestions."

My focus in the program was cemented at the *point* of power every moment of every day. I did the diet and physical work the program suggested to a "T" coupled with an unwavering faith in the process. Then, upon completion of the 12-week challenge program, I let it go and trusted. You see, this is how Source Energy is omnipresent and walks with you. Source Energy within you knows what you want once you have declared your intention. Source Energy also knows where you currently stand in relation to the fulfillment of your desires, and Source also knows the path of least resistance to get you there. What does that mean for you? Rehearse yourself into the belief, as your experiences are based on the thoughts impressed on your subconscious mind. Focus and feel, and this will set the frequency of your vibration to attract back to you that which you are in alignment with. Sensation precedes manifestation and there is no stronger proof than personal experience.

Looking back, the day which came and went that should have brought Bill Philips and I together face-to-face on my driveway as a Top Finisher in my age category was Thursday January 4th, 2001. You know, I was so sure that I was going to win that I even bought the same dress to wear to the celebration gala that the previous year's winner in my age category wore. Trust me, finding that exact dress was the epitome of finding the "needle in the haystack," but I was determined, held the image and I did. On a subconscious level, I had replicated the exact experience of winning my age category detailed right down to the celebration dress. Well you can imagine at first, there was an immense disappointment when I realized it was not meant to be but only for a few moments as I caught a glimpse of my reflection in the mirror. *I had won all right*, I declared. I won myself an amazing physique transformation along with a renewed belief in myself. But, most importantly, I won back an inner deep amount of respect for myself in completing the challenge and holding true to myself-promises.

In the months following, on May 28th, 2001, I received a letter in an odd, small envelope. I pulled out a little card, and after reading the first few words, I was in utter disbelief. I was personally being acknowledged as an overall Top Finisher in the 2000 Body-for-Life Challenge! There were 700,000 people worldwide who entered the challenge—spanning 50 countries—and I placed in the top 2,000.

To put that in perspective, that's in the top 0.30 percentile, less than half of 1%! There were only a few hundred Canadians in the top 2,000. The little card was an invitation to attend a Night of Champions dinner and public photo shoot in Edmonton, Alberta, with Porter Freeman of EAS Sports Nutrition, who was creator Bill Philips's appointed ambassador for the Body-for-Life program.

"Whatever we plant in our subconscious mind and nourish with repetition and emotion will one day become a reality."
—*Earl Nightingale*

So how is it that we wake up one day and hardly recognize the person in the mirror? Well, back in 2000 before engaging in the Body for Life Challenge, I was 36 years old and living in a small town called Teulon, outside of Winnipeg. The gym I attended was a 96-mile return trip commute.

Back then, I worked part-time as a massage therapist in a neighbouring small community and part-time as an administrative director with a massage therapy college in the city. And so it is that I was so committed to my job and to servicing the well-being of others that I completely neglected my own health. It's a familiar trap for many of us. Added to this destructive mix, was a history of low self-esteem and a daunting uncertainty about who I was. This uncertainty stemmed from being adopted at the very young age of 18 months. I had been placed in three separate foster homes and had an additional short stay back with the biological mother all within the tender timeframe of 18 months. Experts agree the first 18 months are some of the most impressionable times for an infant. Why? Let's think back to the workings of our conscious and subconscious minds. The conscious mind, the reasoning mind where we can either accept or reject a thought in the instance of an infant, has had no life experience yet from which to draw contrast. Therefore, what a baby experiences filters directly into the subconscious mind. This is where the foundation of our belief system originates. In my experience during the first 18 months, it was the fear of detachment that bred separation anxiety and low self-esteem later on in life.

This had plagued me for years, although I fought it tirelessly. This affected every aspect of my life.

I had tried the self-help tapes and would ride on the "enthusiasm wagon" for a short while before falling off. I also read books and exercised intermittently, but all the while I was still running on marbles. It was emotionally exhausting, and it became apparent that, like a great boxing match, I was winning a few rounds along the way, but was losing the overall fight. I was repulsed by who I was, and my progressive weight gain validated that. What's worse was that I didn't care to save myself from this vicious self-sabotage cycle. It was like I was absent—even numb to life—though I knew I needed to embrace a sense of self-worth. I knew somewhere deep within, I was worth the fight, as are you.

And so, one gorgeous afternoon, I left work a few minutes early and went to the gym. Mid-afternoon was a great time to go because there were very few people working out. The overall atmosphere at the women's only gym was pleasant with large, bright windows and the smell of disinfectant wafting through the air. Looking as good as it gets during my gym time, I left the change room in my baggy sweats and oversized t-shirt.

First I stopped at the bicep machine where I struggled through a few sets of bicep curls. Looking straight into the mirror, I didn't know who that was staring back at me. Like a total disconnection of self. Next, I was on to the leg extension machine for another few sets. Nine . . . ten . . . eleven . . . twelve and the weight stack came down with a sharp whack that pierced the air as I felt the burn in my thigh muscles. Well, 25 minutes had passed now, and I heard myself whisper aloud, "Good enough, let's go."

I hurried to the change room, but for some strange reason that day I managed to guilt myself to stay an extra few minutes, so I went back to the dumbbell rack to work my shoulders. Again, taking another hard look, I said to the stranger in the mirror, tears rolling down my face, "You are nothing but a reflection of broken self-promises." That truth cut deep emotionally. An emotional cut that I knew would hauntingly repeat itself through an inner echo for several days, even weeks to come.

Out of the corner of my eye, I caught some activity behind me on the aerobic mats—a young woman chatting on her cell phone. How was this even allowed? This was sacred gym time!

Curious though, I kept glancing back. She was strikingly beautiful, like a goddess sculpted to perfection. Long blond hair, blue eyes, perfectly proportioned, and with confidence oozing from her pores. Clad in scandalously cheeky, tight shorts and a white, deep-v tank top that she more than filled, I remember thinking what a stunning woman she was. She was sitting cross-legged in front of the mirrors, talking on the phone, and doing some sort of fluffy sit up.

Then she stood up, and it was like the heavens opened and angels sang "Ahhhhhhh," with the sun's rays illuminating her bronzed body. My gawd! She had the most beautifully sculpted and muscular set of get-away sticks I had ever seen. Like a blinking marquee sign in my head, I remember saying to myself, "I want to look like her!" A staff member wandered over to get her off the phone—I was hoping—but they ended up looking at each other's nails, outfits and runners, and giggling.

After a few minutes, the goddess left the gym area. I looked over at the staff member, made eye contact, and we exchanged this kind of awkward, friendly-like smile. I was so ready to go, but the fear of disrobing in front of the goddess kept me going on a few more machines until I figured it would be safe to go into the change room. I would have preferred enduring the pain of tearing a muscle than undressing in her presence.

On my way, the staff member looked over and said, "Have a great day!" I stopped dead in my tracks, turned and walked over to her. I asked the staff member, "That lady you were just speaking with, what does she do for a training program? She works so little and looks that great!" The staff member threw her head back with a little chuckle and replied, "She's a bikini model, and her secret is Body-for-Life. You can get Body-for-Life at the nutrition store in the mall."

With a cautiously renewed enthusiasm and an "all clear" on the goddess's presence in the change room, I quickly changed and was on my way to the nutrition store. I couldn't get there fast enough. When I arrived, I glanced around and could not see any Body-for-Life bottles. The clerk asked if he could help. I turned to him and said, "I'm looking for the Body-for-Life pill."

He chuckled and walked out from behind the counter. He said, "No Body-for-Life pill that I'm aware of, but we do have the book." I thought, "A book?! I don't want or need another damn book." So I turned on my heels and started to walk out the door. The clerk said, "I hear it's a pretty easy read." I stood for a moment and thought back to the goddess ... I gave him $20.00 and left with my new book.

When I got home, I sat in a comfortable chair in the sunroom, cleared all my skepticism and opened the book. The premise was a 12-week challenge to an inner and physical transformation based on a manageable workout that didn't require a lot of time, coupled with a sensible eating plan. I flipped through the *before and after* photos of individuals who had completed the challenge, read their stories and identified myself with one particular woman who had won overall in our age category the previous year. I read the first few chapters and decided to accept the 12-week challenge. The stakes were too high if I chose to do nothing and stay imprisoned in my old patterns.

It was difficult and awkward at first, as is anything new. I photocopied and cut out a picture of her body that I aspired to look like and tucked it in my purse. I also copied the picture and put one copy on the bathroom mirror and one on the fridge. I made up a calendar on my computer and pre-planned our week's meals. My husband, Dennis, and I worked on this together and wrote out breakfast, snack, lunch and supper meals. The program was easy to follow as there were sample meal suggestions and a list of Nutrition-for-Life authorized foods laid out in the book. I began to feel a shift. I was beginning to take control. Dennis and I planned our trips to the grocery store, knew exactly what we needed, and didn't deviate from this—no matter the cravings and tendency to want *just one* treat. It was a choice and every day was a new challenge, a blank slate.

I was learning that no matter how many decisions a person makes in a moment, an hour, a day, a week or a month, those choices are sculpting the person you are today. The decisions you make must resonate authentically with you and light up your inner being, so you shine outwardly and glow for the world to embrace and to inspire; this gives permission to others to live their lives authentically.

To help keep me on track with the ups, downs and deviations we all experience because of our external environments, on a blank 4 × 6 piece of paper, I wrote the letter W, and on another piece of paper I wrote L. Every morning I would lie in bed and assess how I was feeling overall before my feet hit the floor. If I felt good and optimistic about conquering the day with directed intent, I would get the W, which stood for a *winning* day. I carried it with me in my purse, and if I felt I was about to waiver from my self-promise, I would pull it out and remind myself of all the positive feelings I had that day and previous days and how grateful I was to have the gift of life at that particular moment.

Equally important was the L card. If I was feeling low, I accepted this and went about my day granting myself permission to be who I needed to be that day. In those times, my mind was not in a positive space, or my body was out of sorts. We all need to be okay with these days and be kind to ourselves. This allows whatever void to begin to heal in a pressure-free environment. You owe that to yourself.

Being hard on yourself isn't the answer. Loving yourself is. Your self-love sets you free to be the beautiful person you are. It's your time.

A few weeks into my program, my husband bought me a workout shirt that read *Under Construction*. These two words inspired and reminded me that I was embarking on a journey, not a final destination. It reminded me that I didn't have to be perfect in the moment, not now, not ever, but that all aspects of my life were under construction, which shed a new, never-before-permitted way of thinking about my faults. This discovery and way of thinking mined the realization that some of my faults were actually the catalysts in revealing my new path to interpersonal and spiritual growth.

Every week, I was setting new goals, planning new meals, reflecting on past accomplishments and embracing the power of visualization.

As life will throw in unexpected curve balls just when we think we've mastered momentum, sadly in Week 6, while pulling into the parking lot at the gym, my cell phone rang.

A soft, choked voice at the other end said, "Daphne? This is a good friend of Darren's, and I'm calling to let you know he has passed suddenly."

Darren was a work associate I had an extreme respect for. A very funny man who was so severely disabled, he could only walk with the assistance of two canes. In that moment, as his image flashed on the screen of my mind, I could feel my eyes well up with tears, and the lump in my throat expanded. I was shattered.

I turned the car off and cried. After a few minutes, I wiped the tears and made a promise that from then on, all lower body workouts were dedicated to Darren. I was sad yet honoured that our paths had crossed during his short life, as I had learned a lot about human struggle from him though he never complained. I knew he could never exercise his legs and feel the joy of an exhilarating workout, so in honour of his special life, together in Spirit we worked our legs and accomplished astonishing results! Change the meaning, change your life.

At the conclusion of the 12-week challenge, my entire being had transformed into a beautiful tapestry of contentment, which radiated into my marriage, family and work life. I could feel my heart was light, and I felt a long-awaited reconnection to my authentic self. I was excited! At long last, I knew I had begun the journey I was destined to take.

The Night of Champions gala was a remarkable experience and left me with a humble yet overwhelming feeling of accomplishment. All those decisions and choices had accumulated to this spectacular reward. At dinner that night, Porter

Freeman looked at me and asked, "Daphne, what's next for you?" I thought to myself, *How could I top this?* I replied that since I was 15 years old I had always wanted to be a bodybuilder, and in that moment, I told Porter that I was going to compete in a bodybuilding competition. But deep down, I did not really believe what I was saying to him.

As we finished our dinner and lively conversations with the other Top Finishers, Porter handed me an autographed photo of himself. At the bottom he wrote, "Daphne, You've already won! ~ Porter." Whammo!

Those three words—written as though I was coming *from* the place of already being an accomplished and decorated bodybuilder—resonated, and the seed was firmly planted. I felt the nudge, and I knew exactly what was next. Recall that Source is always for expansion and fuller expression. It was my time.

My success story caught the attention of a newspaper journalist in the city. She wanted to interview me for her Active Living column. We made arrangements to meet and I sat with her in a small coffee shop, showed her my before and after photos, shared my story and she was amazed by the transformation.

On July 9, 2001, my story was told in a half-page article in the *Winnipeg Free Press* including my before and after photos and the headline, "Woman Exalts in Body-for-Life." This was a personal accomplishment and a huge honour. Never had I thought it would unfold to this scale. My success was the result of a string of decisions over a sustained period, coupled with triumphing over challenges. It all stemmed from a desire to make a change.

MONDAY, JULY 9, 2001

Winnipeg Free Press

Woman exalts in Body for Life

Eating, exercise program brings quick results

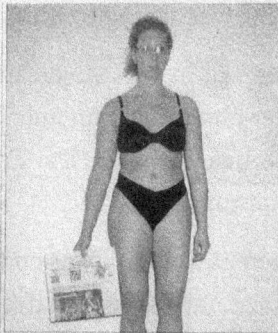

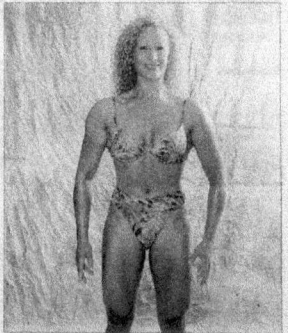

Daphne Sheppard poses for the classic before and after photographs she had taken for her entry in the transformation challenge.

'I finally realize I can achieve anything I dream of'

— Daphne Sheppard

Figure 1 *Credit: Winnipeg Free Press and Shamona Harnett ~ July 9, 2001*

I want you to close your eyes for a moment and think of the analogy of an electrocardiogram. In our example here, the ECG machine will demonstrate your personal lifeline and your decisions along the way. The thrill of accomplishment, overcoming the challenges and embracing life in all its splendour are the upward peaks or positive inflections, and the downward movements represent the necessary annoyances of day-to-day living and the very real-to-life, negative, crisis-type deflections. Those are the circumstances that cause us to derail. The third and last reading on our ECG machine is what is called a flat line. It is a time-sequence measurement that shows no activity. If it is not addressed quickly, you suffer permanent damage or pass away.

Now, let's discuss for a moment the law of opposites, also known as the law of polarity, which decrees that everything has its pair of opposites; opposites are identical in nature but can differ in degree. In other words, there are two sides to everything (for example, there cannot be an in without an out, an up without a down, a front without a back, hot without cold, light without darkness, good without evil or positive without negative). So it makes perfect sense that on our lifeline, we cannot have positive inflections without some negative deflections. Take a deep breath here because this alleviates for us the struggle of striving for and maintaining a consistency in excellence and perfection, for it does not exist! Where there is failure, there has to be success—the polar opposite. In an upward spike of triumph or accomplishment, there has had to be some downward deflection. Understanding this simple truth is liberating. Isn't it?

When we flat line, there is no activity. If we are not creating, we are disintegrating. Understand that all our failures are learning experiences and contain the seeds to success. What is most important is what we are learning in our experiences along the way.

Be grateful for what you have today, and in the present tense write out what you are grateful for that you have already achieved. These are your desires and most daring and fanciful dreams as follows in this example:

"I am so happy and grateful **now** that . . ." Write in the present tense. For example, I would write, "I am so happy and grateful now that I am in high demand as a successful motivational speaker making an impactful difference in the lives of my worldwide audiences and so it is. Thank you, Spirit."

You must become emotionally attached to that which you desire. Your eyes are the windows to your soul, and you have to see it already in your possession utilizing the magnificence of your imagination. In Body-for-Life, remember that my intent and outcome were so clear that I even purchased my celebration dress. You have to feel it, smell, taste and hear what it is like. Why? Because your subconscious mind cannot tell the difference between you merely thinking the thought of acquiring your desire and actually being in possession of it. Once you impress this notion upon your subconscious mind, your body becomes that physical tuning fork in vibration with Source Energy that is omnipresent, and you will attract that with which you are in harmony. This is again the workings of the law of attraction. It is your call-out to the universe to align and harmonize that which you desire and want to experience in your current reality.

This is where the magic was in Porter's comment, about already winning the bodybuilding competition. In my mind, I had already won and was already in receipt of the multiple trophies I earned before even setting foot on stage. Cultivate an attitude of gratitude, and focus your attention on the goodness in your life today and what you want to attract to you. Our consciousness allows us the ability to choose with free will and with faith based on the understanding of the precise laws in which our universe operates, will illuminate your path to a life of prosperity, manifestation and abundance. Stay focused, see through your heart, and stay seated in gratitude as the universe is always working in your favour, regardless of appearance and current circumstance.

Let's start making small, daily decisions that peak our upward and positive inflections and understand that the negative deflections are necessary in our pursuit. It's your time!

Activating your Brilliance—Points to Ponder

1) Moving forward into today, we need to understand that we cannot let any of the negative events of yesterday, last week, last month or last year leech into the gift of our new day ~ today. It's about choice, your choice. Journal and give thanks for the lessons learned yesterday.

2) Rehearse yourself into the belief, as your physical experiences are based on the thoughts impressed on your subconscious mind. Focus and feel, and this will set the frequency of your vibration to attract back to you that which you are in alignment with. Sensation precedes manifestation.

3) It makes perfect sense that on our lifeline, we cannot have positive inflections without negative deflections. Take a deep breath here because this alleviates the struggle for us in our daily tasks of striving for and maintaining a consistency in excellence and perfection, for it does not exist!

Chapter Five

The DNA of Your Success

$\mathcal{M}$y formula is a little longer than some of the other success formulas you may see, but I find it is all encompassing.

Desire + Commitment + Consistency / Results–Negativity = Fulfilled Living

Let's break this down. A desire to make a change—no matter how small—must exist first. In the last chapter, I talked about how repulsed I was, and I didn't know who that was staring back at me in the mirror at the gym. I knew something had to change. I was very uncomfortable in life.

For the longest time, my life was analogous to a pot of boiling water. Bubbling and simmering just below the lip of the pot causing the lid to pop up once in a while, but mostly simmering keeping the lid dancing on the lip of the pot.

That day in the gym was the painful acknowledgement and burning truth that I did not matter to myself anymore. There was that much self-hate, and I felt empty and spiritually depleted. How and why did I allow that to happen? I knew a lot of it stemmed from the adoption, but I had absolutely no idea how to fix it. This was extremely frustrating, and I was infuriated, and it was the power of those emotions that caused the boiling water to spill over and overturn the lid.

This was the tipping point, and somewhere deep inside; I sensed it was my time. You, too, will know your boiling point, as it will be different in each of us. Some common internal dialogue that will confirm your frustration may sound like:

"I've had it."

"I can't take this anymore."

"This is it."

"I can't go on like this."

Once the desire has been identified or established, you must cultivate it. Your desire is what you feel inspired to do, and this is that core truth that resonates within your heart space. The very essence of who you are will breathe life into your desires. Understand that desires are not just fleeting thoughts of "I hope to" but rather you are eternally connected to them. This is where the process can go south for a lot of people. Your desire must be unwavering. It is detrimental to your overall well-being to stay in one place, your commonplace that feels comfortable to you when ultimately the core of your being desires otherwise. This struggle within you is not serving you spiritually, emotionally or physically. It's like a Ferrari that is renowned and built for racing but instead is stuck in a puddle of mud spinning, not getting anywhere except dirty and carboned up. Too much of this toxic build-up will lead to an array of instabilities psychologically identified as feelings of doubt, worry or anxiety which can lead to ill effects physiologically over time. This is a state of dis-ease within. The equivalent emotions are that of chaos, sadness and generally out-of-sorts. It can also be the beginning of self-medicating with your weapon of choice: food, alcohol, drugs or other impulsive behaviours.

Once you have established your desires and you feel that flood of elation within that comes from the integration of a seamless bond between what it is you desire and your core truth, commit to not cheating yourself, commit to knowing that you are worthy, and commit to honouring your promises to yourself. Your life is not a dress rehearsal. We are on stage right now, starring in the performance of our lives every day. Don't be an extra in your own movie. Life is in the now, time is precious, and you owe it to yourself to give life to and fulfill the desires you know have been simmering inside . . . Trust that you will be rewarded for living a life of authenticity.

In this moment now, commit. Commit to loving who you are. Commit to the process. Be kind, and love yourself. Take the step and commit. It's your time.

The commitment to honour every fabric in your tapestry of self, in every moment, every day and every week forward, will be the greatest gift you give yourself and those around you. As a side note here, a gift is also known as a present. Is that purely coincidence? Be your gift; be present in your pursuit. Consistency is the third element of my formula and serves as a repetition of the commitment to yourself. It is what etches the message or behaviour you desire to make upon your subconscious mind. Desire + commitment (to the cultivation of) + consistency.

Once you've pioneered your way and begun to feel the empowering change, you will start to feel the magic. Take the time to reflect back, acknowledge and celebrate the progress you've made—it is fuel for the journey. Write it out. Are there going to be setbacks? As sure as the sun will come up tomorrow—that's just life. And when that happens, look back at your notes, take a sturdy stance and proclaim, "It's MY time."

Now whatever you do, don't let circumstance rob you of this. If circumstance or an unwanted external experience has an ironclad hold on you and puts you in a tailspin, acknowledge and surrender that it is happening for a reason. That reason may not be clear at the time, or in a week or a year. Make the decision, the choice, in that moment to restore some control so that you are not completely swept away and set adrift. It could very well be a circumstantial nudge that is setting you on a path, a little "tweak" along the way. Manage the time as you are best able. Grow, learn and increase your awareness of self through the circumstance or journey, as there is a lesson. It is never time lost. Time would only be lost if you lose the lesson.

Results are wonderful things. They are the fruits of your efforts manifested into form. They are your new platform from which your next journey will begin. Life is an ascending staircase to the heavens. One step up takes you to a new height, a new perspective on which you conceive and breathe life into your next desire. Protect your ascent by acknowledging any pessimism or negativity you feel along the way, externally or from within. Be attuned to where it is originating. Is the source old beliefs that originated in the environment where you grew up? If it is not serving you in any way, then let it go immediately. Don't give it another second of your precious, beautiful and meaningful life. Weed out negativity; there is no place for it in your abundant garden of life.

Negativity is all around us. It is my personal choice to refrain from watching TV, with the exception of a few chosen programs that inspire me. The following is a glimpse into my garden of thought and is what resonates true for me. My deliberate vibrational frequency or my vibe has brought much joy and success to my life. As a real estate agent, I enjoy watching *Home and Garden TV* and *Million Dollar Listing* for a relaxing, light evening at home. Another show I love watching is *America's Got Talent* for the sheer inspiration I feel watching some of the contestants. Where they came from, their dreams, their desires, their struggles and then, for some, their joyous, triumphant emotion of "making it" to the finals. I often shed tears of joy as they share their true-life stories. I feel their passion, their vibration that gives me goose bumps. These are ordinary people from all walks and backgrounds with extraordinary talent. Everyone has a story in them. I also refrain from reading the newspaper but will glance at it from time to time just to keep abreast of local and national headlines. I choose instead to keep rooted in my purpose, which is to inspire and love, as I believe expressions of love are overdue. It is my practice to express daily gratitude for my life and for the lives of others whom I meet—one Spirit, one conversation at a time. It is my purpose to serve and to contribute, which I believe is the essence of life.

I also believe that by focusing on those closest to me, imparting an impression that they are beautiful spiritual beings with purpose, is what makes the experiences in my life so rich: the love and peace they feel will reflect openly to help mend our world. And as my circle of influence grows, the love and light continues to cast outwards in an ever-increasing circle, a ripple effect.

It all starts here. I see it this way: one musical instrument alone can make beautiful music but when accompanied by other instruments in an orchestrated environment, that gives rise to a sensational, uplifting experience. The strings, brass, woodwinds, keyboards and percussives produce a magnificent depth of sound complemented by their community of surrounding instruments. The overall exquisite sound vibrations resonate, are felt by the audience, and an emotional connection ensues. At the conclusion of a seamless performance, there is a standing ovation—a cooperative, enthusiastic outburst of positive emotion within that close circle of influence, the audience. Each guest departs the concert hall, richly impacted by the experience and tells others, and so the ripple effect goes. We all have a role to play in the world growing friendlier, more welcoming, more loving and more peaceful.

It's our mandate to shine as children do, and to exist with a positive, nourishing light with like-minded people. One of my favourite quotes from Marianne Williamson, which I carry around in a plastic sleeve in my purse, goes as follows:

> "Our deepest fear is not that we are inadequate. Our deepest fear is that we are powerful beyond measure. It is our light, not our darkness, that most frightens us.
>
> "We ask ourselves, who am I to be brilliant, gorgeous, talented, fabulous? Actually, who are you not to be? You are a child of God. Your playing small does not serve the

world. There is nothing enlightening about shrinking so that other people won't feel insecure around you. We are all meant to shine, as children do. We were born to make manifest the glory of God, that is within us. It's not just in some of us; it's in everyone. And as we let our light shine, we unconsciously give other people permission to do the same. As we are liberated from our own fear, our presence automatically liberates others."

—Marianne Williamson from her book "*A Return to Love*"

And so, be phenomenal, follow your heart's desire, and design a life of abundance. Be amazing, and never say never. Be authentic, and live true to your purpose. Be loving and kind, and always leave everyone with the impression of increase. Be generous, and the law of attraction dictates that is exactly what will come back to you. Be creative, and always remember that you are the miracle. This is truly life fulfilled. . . . It's your time!

Activating your Brilliance—Points to Ponder

1) Your desire is what you feel inspired to do, and this is the truth that resonates within your heart space. The very essence of who you are breathes life into your desires. Don't be an extra in your own movie.

2) Once you have established your desires and you feel that flood of elation within that comes from the integration of a seamless bond between what it is you desire and your core truth, commit to not cheating yourself, commit to knowing that you are worthy and commit to honouring your promises to yourself.

". . . we ask ourselves, who am I to be brilliant, gorgeous, talented, fabulous? Actually, who are you not to be?"
—*Marianne Williamson*

Chapter Six

The Power of Visualization: The Mind's Eye

*W*e have embarked on this journey to better understand the concept of energy within our minds, body and Spirit and our purpose within our world. It is also my hope for you that you better understand how we are co-creators with Source Energy and how the law of attraction works. So, the time has come to discover the power of visualization; that is my second personal story. This is an example of how powerful visualization can be almost beyond belief. Know that you have the potential already within you. It is just waiting for your sanction. The image you cast on the screen of your mind accompanied with the alignment to that desire could produce extraordinary results in every aspect of your life. Once again, nothing resonates as truth like personal experience. Here we go . . .

In the late 1980s, there was a magazine called *Women's Physique World*. I loved to flip through the pages of some of the world's bodybuilding greats showcasing their physiques, including Carla Dunlap, Bev Francis, Kay Baxter and Rachel McLish.

These women were the great bodybuilding pioneers. They were determined to carve a path in the highly male-dominated sport. Not only were they re-defining the sport, but they also struggled with the public's perception of women having muscular mass. I was in awe of their tenacity, persistence, razor focus and unbeatable commitment to make their mark in history.

Fast forward 28 years, and women today are admired and adorned for their athleticism in fitness competitions, their hard and musculature physiques in bodybuilding, figure and bikini competitions at prestigious events like the Arnold Classic and International Federation of Bodybuilding Ms. Olympia Competition, within their communities and divisions worldwide.

There was one bodybuilder, though, who really caught my attention. Her name was Cory Everson. She was not only beautiful but was sculpted and hard, with perfect muscle proportion and symmetry unlike any other.

In 1987, in one of my cherished editions of *Women's Physique World*, I tore out a picture of Cory standing on the tips of her toes, feet shoulder-width apart, with her hands resting on her hips. I kept that photo of her because of my sheer admiration for her physique, and tucked it away in an envelope hoping that *someday* . . .

I still have that photo. After I accomplished my transformation in the Body-for-Life Challenge, recall that I had a conversation with Porter, the ambassador for the challenge, prior to our departure from Edmonton. The seed had been planted in my mind through his comment on the autographed picture that *I'd already won*. I say *planted* because even when I spoke to Porter that evening, the words "I am going to compete in a bodybuilding competition" were just running off my tongue, vacant of a plan. I was 37 years old and had never worked out with a plan or goal to become a bodybuilder.

When we arrived home from Edmonton, and life was returning to its regular rhythms, I put that signed photo of Porter that said, "Daphne, You've already won" downstairs in our small, workout room. The next few years were filled with just doing stuff: life on autopilot with no immediate plan. Life was good, but without establishing written goals working toward competing in bodybuilding, I was absent of a life script, absent of direction. The pages and chapters in my *Book of Life*, which I talk about later on in Chapter 10, were largely blank. Days turned into weeks, weeks into months and the desire to follow through with competitive bodybuilding faded. I was content passing time by working, occasionally working out, enjoying different wines, with a vague effort to try to eat healthy. I had not committed to the conscious decision to create that bodybuilding reality for myself. I had no direction and instead allowed the circumstantial *current of life* take me to uncharted, meaningless and unwanted territory, drifting farther and farther from the goal of "someday." In short, I had succumbed to the dreaded "comfort zone."

As the months passed, I knew it was time for a path correction, when I was challenged with the reality of having to buy a few sizes up in clothing. This was the alarm, a.k.a. that circumstantial nudge that meant things were way out of hand, that it was time to re-assess. As the extra weight started to accumulate, it was time again for a decision. I felt as though I was suffocating my attempt to live a fulfilled life, a life authentic to my purpose and expression that was uniquely mine as it was being choked by the blah, blah, blah of daily living in the comfort zone and by the empty decisions I was making along the way. I was *merely existing* and reacting to circumstance as a lot of us seem to do.

It was the spring of 2004, and the Manitoba Novice Bodybuilding Competition was just around the corner. I ordered my ticket and attended the show on Saturday, March 19th, 2004. If you are in search of motivation to transform your physique, I highly recommend attending your local bodybuilding association show! You will light up with renewed enthusiasm, no matter your goal. This is exactly what happened to me that Saturday. The weather was beginning to turn with the promise of summer in the air. People were out and about, coughing the dust out of their lungs after a long winter cooped up indoors. I felt the excitement and energy in the auditorium that day for it was palpable and knew that it was my time.

When I got home, I wrote a page and a half documenting what had just transpired, both at the competition and the previous 34 months of drifting aimlessly. Though I maliciously wanted to turn within and blame myself for wasting time, I adhered to my vow to love myself, no matter the outcome, and immediately established boundaries. Rule #1, I didn't blame myself but rather chalked it up to circumstance. I also realized that now was my time to establish and shape a new path with new decisions. Rule #2, I wasn't going to let the past define me or have any bearing on my future endeavours. What was, was and the point of power was at that moment! Then the ah ha moment; the nudge—I remembered that picture of Cory Everson. Where was it? I searched for two days, inside the house, outside in the shed and in the garage. Day two of my frantic search, I returned to the shed and started to move some of the same boxes aggressively again on the top shelf between the Christmas decorations and motorcycle parts. There, pasted flat against the wall, most likely from the freeze/thaw of several seasons past, the manila envelope appeared. I opened it carefully, and there she was—with a few other miscellaneous magazine photos and keepsakes.

First thing, I had the magazine page with her photograph laminated, as it was starting to look its age. My visual goal had been set. My competition goal was also set: to compete in the Manitoba Novice Bodybuilding Competition the next year, in 2005. I had no idea how much weight I had to lose, but I didn't care. My sights were set on *looking like* Cory Everson, nothing less!

So, I knew in my mind's eye what I was going to look like, plus I had the positive message from Porter, plus the experience and energy I felt at the local bodybuilding competition I attended. Why then, did it take me from March of that year until July to act? The answer? I fell victim to a well-known phenomenon called the "knowing-doing gap," which plagues many of us throughout our lifetime. We know what we want to do, however, we don't act, and it can be very frustrating, but is not uncommon. It's easy to lose sight of the bigger picture and stay in our comfort zone. Just as I had. In my example, I knew exactly what I wanted to do, I had a visual goal and a date. From my success formula in the previous chapter, I had the desire but was lacking in other elements. I had not taken any action to commit to the process, merely surface talked about it. Without the actual commitment to take action, there were no physical workouts to measure against the other element in my success formula—consistency/results. The other hurdle was the negative self-talk. . . . "Who are you to think that, after all these years, you might actually pull this off? You're too old. People are going to laugh." This evoked fear, doubt and worry, which put me in a negative state or negative vibration and stopped me cold in my tracks. I recognized though, like kindling is to a fire, deep within me there was still a burning desire to compete.

I feel it's important here to delve a little further into understanding the dynamics and our responsibility in diverting the "knowing-doing gap." All in all, we are creatures of habit. We do things a certain way, and these repetitive activities (habits) have etched and defined a track in our subconscious mind. Then, autonomy of the activity/habit sets in. In this analogy, I'm going to ask you to think of an old vinyl record. There are minute grooves over the surface; when the needle is placed upon them, they play the record, and you hear the music. Wherever you place the needle on the record, you will consistently hear those specific notes and lyrics of the song. Let's begin to put this into perspective of our lives. The grooves are your habits, etched in your subconscious mind. Every time the needle (or a thought) comes in contact with the grooves (your habits/patterning), a specific part of the song (carried out) will be heard (outcome). For example, if

I gave you a bicycle, it is through your past, repetitive conditioning, etched in your subconscious mind, that you are easily able to engage in a physical series of actions that enable you to get the bicycle moving without thinking of all the multitude of steps that are occurring simultaneously to do so.

And so, to eliminate or disrupt our habitual defaults, we have to decide consciously and take the necessary action to scratch the surface of the record to interrupt the grooves, so they cannot be replayed. It is then that we can consciously create and introduce new thoughts, new behaviours and entrench (habitualize) new grooves on our subconscious mind that play a different tune. We bridge the gap with a new set of behaviours that knits us to the goals we had established for our desired outcome.

Well, like a fine recipe; I had most of the ingredients, but I lacked direction and belief in myself. The outcome of this recipe was destined to be a flop, and that is exactly what had happened. I spun in my tracks for three months (from March to June), paralyzed by the life-experience-robbing Gremlins. I was frustrated because precious time was passing. In my head, all the competitors that I would stand on stage with in the months ahead were already well on their way to their competition bodies. This played in my mind almost every waking moment, and I finally came to the conclusion that I would experience more pain in the sheer disappointment in myself if I did not take the leap of faith and at least try than if I did compete and nothing came out of it. I knew, later in life I would have had the "I wish I would have" talk with myself, and I couldn't bear the thought of that! I had learned from my previous lessons to honour my self-promise.

And so, the next step perhaps was the most significant and the key to my success. With the desired end in mind, meaning I was coming from the place of already having competed, I sat down in a quiet environment, took a piece of paper and wrote the following:

"I have decided to make a change and take full responsibility and to move forward from where I am physically and my state of health today. My reasons are many: I don't feel good. I'm unhappy and feel like my energy in life is mediocre. My clothes don't fit me, and I feel embarrassed, which then turns to anger because I am the only one to blame. By accepting my current reality, I am taking the control back in my life, and it feels empowering and great! I want to glow and feel like the vibrant, young woman I'm supposed to be. Because I can!"

Objective/Goal:

1) To compete March 2005 heavyweight bodybuilding competition.

2) In three months, get weight to 170 (October 8th).

3) In early December—weight to 155 lbs.

I had reached the proverbial boiling point, did my research and made a phone call. In other words, I took action.

I had been given the name of a part-time trainer, who was also a natural bodybuilder. This was very important to me, as I was 40 years old and not about to introduce enhancement aids in my quest for my Cory Everson physique. We had a challenge, though, that we discovered in our initial phone conversation. He lived 1½ hours away and wanted to see me 3 × per week. There was no way I could commit to this financially or from the perspective of the commute. However, I was ultimately committed to the process. We decided that we would try 1× per month, but we knew that this was less than optimal for my ultimate goal and that I must promise not to cheat, to stay persistent in my training and true to my self-promises.

My first sit down session with him was Friday, July 9th, 2004 at 2:00 pm. Do you know why I remember this date and time so clearly? Well, he wanted to see me in a two-piece bathing suit in his house, under a spotlight, and I was tipping the scales at 200 lbs. Sheesh! Time was of the essence, however. The competition date was March 19th, 2005, a mere 36 weeks away to stage day.

The first thing I did was run off monthly calendars from July 2004 through to March 2005. On the first month, I wrote right on the front of the calendar page my goals/objectives and highlighted them in orange. The next step, I flipped to March 19th, 2005, and noted the competition day, and filled that day in with yellow highlighter. I counted the days backward and wrote them in all the squares, the countdown. I found this a very effective visual tool in gauging my time invested versus my results. It prompted me to step it up a notch if my progress wasn't where it should be to meet my final weight goal. Due to the nature of the dieting involved, the next step was to write in all the birthday commitments, barbecues and social events, so that I could plan ahead, prepare and package my food to take to the event to ward off any likelihood of getting side-tracked.

Next was the exercise component. I knew I had to do a lot of cardio, and I wrote in five of seven days a week to do that. Rest days were also important days, and were recorded with a little happy face in the respective calendar squares. The body part I was to train was written in as far in advance as the overall training schedule would allow. This was dependent on my spotlight visits with the trainer, though, and where he felt I needed improvement.

Voila! My direction was crystal clear. No uncertainty, no guess work, just a clearly defined timeline and script. I made notes about my eating habits and progress along the way in the daily calendar squares. I was far from perfect. Written in some of the squares was "terrible eating," "feel horrid," "dead tired," "four licorice sticks." Some squares said "down 6 lbs and one size," "excellent eating," "great leg workout," "awesome shoulder workout," and the odd happy face sprinkled across the pages.

Let's step back for a moment. There is a pattern in these two stories—the Body-for-Life and preparation for the body-building competition that is not uncommon. Do you see the similarities? In both circumstances, I came from a place where I was not in harmony with my truth, which ultimately triggered the incentive for me to establish and set a goal. In both cases, I festered until I reached a "boiling point" that drove me to taking action. Finally, once I made the commitment and my intent was crystal clear, this was followed by deliberate action and extraordinary results unfolded.

When it comes time for you to manifest your dream into reality, and your desire to do so is insistent, you are in exactly the right place and need to act. Recognize the insistency as one of life's pokes and move; take the first step. The universe likes speed. Dwelling on something without doing anything about it will only outdistance you from the unfolding of your reality, from living the life of your dreams. Like the canoe that drifts farther from the shoreline, helpless against the ebb and flow of the restless sea. Don't worry how it will unfold; just take action. Drop your anchor, and the way will be shown to you. It's your time.

The next phase was to start thinking about my stage presence. I checked with the executive director of the provincial bodybuilding association, and he made a few excellent suggestions. We also talked in length about the whole competition process and day. Through his recommendation, I found a company that was willing to make my posing suit. My favourite colour is purple, and with their expertise we worked together to create my suit anticipating my body size and shape for competition day. After eagerly waiting five weeks, the day came when I received the notice that a package had arrived and went to pick it up at the post office in town.

I waited until I got it home, so that I could savour and take pleasure in the moment, with no distractions. After all, this was the first tangible item I had that marked my true commitment to standing on stage on competition day. The package just made it that much more real.

Fumbling with excitement, I opened the package and was horrified! I dropped it on the bed and started to cry. I phoned the executive director and asked if I could come and see him. He was a very accommodating and patient man and told me to come right away. I trekked to Winnipeg, sat down in his office, and advised him that I had had a change of mind and would not be competing.

He was surprised and asked why. I told him that the suit had arrived in a sandwich bag. That's right …. two pieces in a 6 × 6½-inch sandwich bag! The suit top was comprised of two small triangles, no padding with a long string running through them (albeit, a very pretty purple). The bottom looked hardly big enough to cover my cat's bum. I said to him, there was no way I could get on stage in public in that! He laughed. We talked a long while that day, and he was able to put it in perspective for me. He said, "Daphne, as we sit here now, it is definitely hard to imagine wearing this suit, and yes it would stand out. However, on competition day at your competition weight, everyone, all competitors will be wearing similar suits." He advised that I should just set it aside, focus on my training, and that everything would be just fine. That day, he was successful in diverting my setback by changing my perspective about the suit, and I was back to my quest to compete. Change the meaning; change your life.

In December, the final preparations for the competition began. I was approximately 16 weeks out, and it was time to up the cardio, tighten up the diet (no more cheat days) and switch up the weight lifting/body part/split workout schedule. It was a ruthless challenge, and oddly, I loved every minute of it because it demonstrated inner strengths I didn't know existed. In addition, it resonated with my core desires and truth. A commitment that involved persistence, dedication and strength to say no to most foods and all alcohol; strength in honouring my vision and dream; strength in commitment;

strength in allowing the change to occur, which meant actually welcoming uncertainty; strength in trusting the process; strength in enduring pain and physical exhaustion, yet still finding that "get up and go" from deep within. Knowing that there were others that I would soon meet going through the exact same experience.

It is not the purpose of this book to provide you with diet advice. However, I will tell you that my diet for those months was simple. My focus was razor sharp, and I understood that while training, food was no longer to be *enjoyed* but rather food served a fundamental purpose: to nourish my body for optimized growth. I ate a combination of seven to eight basic foods on a daily basis. Tuna, ground bison, chicken breasts, broccoli, oatmeal or rice, and egg whites. And I drank water and protein shakes. I enjoyed cottage cheese with sliced strawberries at bedtime and one cup of black coffee in the morning pre-cardio. I drank lots of water, used no salt or any other condiments. Nada. I was allowed either one cheat day per week (Saturday or Sunday) or one cheat meal spread out over Friday, Saturday and Sunday. A cheat meal for me was usually pancakes with syrup in the morning and a nice steak dinner out with Dennis. No alcohol, not even a chocolate with an alcohol infused centre.

My workouts were nothing short of gruelling. When I started in July, I could only do six sit-ups, so I knew there was a lot of work to do. Most of my weight training was purposely done with my eyes closed and wearing a large, loose t-shirt in my workout room in the basement. The picture of Cory Everson was branded on the screen of my mind, and I did not need the distraction of critiquing my current undesirable physique, which was the reason for the large, loose t-shirt. Every muscle contraction I fought for, I visualized Cory's arm or Cory's leg, shoulders or back when I did my lifting. I visualized my muscle belly filling with blood rich in nutrients to accommodate the micro-tearing and new growth of muscle tissue. I was in the business of building mass.

On March 19th, 2005, at the age of 41, I took stage in front of a sold out audience. With tears welling up in my eyes as I write this, I can tell you it was one of the most amazing and exhilarating experiences of my life! I was humbled with gratitude when presented with three trophies at the conclusion of the evening placing first in my weight class, second in Masters and placing first overall as Best Poser.

Figure 2 *Cory, Women's Physique World,* 1987

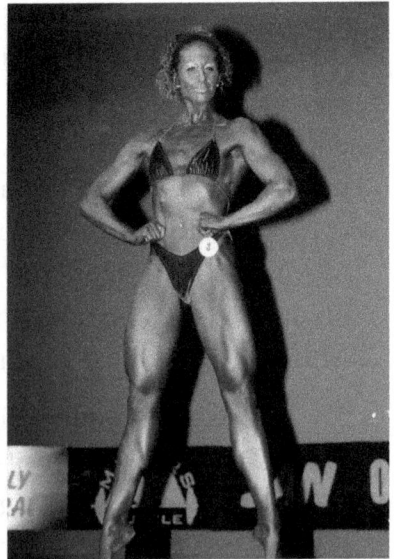

Figure 3 *Daphne, Bodybuilding Competition,* 2005

During that competition and my routine that night, a photographer took a picture of a pose I held for just a moment. When I received the photograph a few weeks later, I could not believe my eyes! My trainer could not believe his eyes. I have included the photos below following a mere 36 weeks of training, and it is a personal testament that visualization and motor imaging of your desires and goals is a very powerful tool.

Well, on March 26th, 2005, one week following the competition, my trainer encouraged me to compete in the Provincials that year. So I printed out March, April, May and June calendars and mapped out the timeline. On Saturday, June 18th, I competed in the provincial bodybuilding competition, winning an additional two trophies and a berth to compete in the Canadian National Bodybuilding Competition in August. My trainer was ecstatic and couldn't wait to get me onto the next level of his diet and exercise. However, after a few seconds of contemplation, I respectfully declined.

I was deeply honoured and grateful about my success and journey at the completion of the provincial competition, but I knew it was time to open and receive the next gentle nudge life had in store for me.

In my studies on the Law of Attraction, I came across this very relevant citation on the power of visualization, and I want to share it with you here. In 1921, Genevieve Behrend, a student of the late Thomas Troward, wrote about *Your Invisible Power,* and in the first chapter she perhaps best explains the "Order of Visualization" as follows:

"The exercise of the visualizing faculty keeps your mind in order and attracts to you the things you need to make life more enjoyable in an orderly way. If you train yourself in practice of deliberately picturing your desire and carefully examining your picture, you will soon find that your thoughts and desires proceed in a more orderly procession than ever before. Having reached a state of ordered mentality, you are no longer in a constant state of mental hurry. Hurry is Fear, and consequently destructive.

In other words, when your understanding grasps the power to visualize your heart's desire and hold it with your will, it attracts to you all things requisite to the fulfillment of that picture by the harmonious vibrations of the law of attraction. You realize that since order is Heaven's first law, and visualization places things in their natural order, then it must be a heavenly thing to visualize.

Everyone visualizes, whether he knows it or not. Visualizing is the great secret of success. The conscious use of this great power attracts to you multiplied resources, intensifies your wisdom, and enables you to make use of advantages which you formerly failed to recognize....

We now fly through the air, not because anyone has been able to change the laws of nature but because the inventor of the flying machine learned how to apply nature's laws and, by making orderly use of them, produced the desired result. So far as natural forces are concerned, nothing has changed since the beginning. There were no airplanes in the Year One, because those of that generation could not conceive the idea as a practical working possibility. "It has not yet been done" was the argument, "and it cannot be done." Yet the laws and materials for practical flying machines existed then as now.

Troward tells us that the great lesson he learned from the airplane and wireless telegraphy is the triumph of principle over precedent, the working of an idea to its logical conclusion, in spite of accumulated contrary testimony of all past experience.

With such an example before you, you must realize that there are still greater secrets to be disclosed. You hold the key within yourself with which to unlock the secret chamber that contains your heart's desire. All that is necessary in order that you may use this key and make your life exactly what you wish it to be is a careful inquiry into the unseen causes which stand back of every external and visible condition. Then bring these unseen causes into harmony with your conception, and you will find that you can make practical working realities of possibilities, which at present seem but fantastic dreams.

In visualizing, or making a mental picture, you are not endeavouring to change the laws of nature. You are fulfilling them.

Your object in visualizing is to bring things into regular order, both mentally and physically. When you realize that this method of employing the creative power brings your desires, one after another, into practical, material accomplishment, your confidence in the mysterious but unfailing law of attraction, which has its central power station in the very heart of your word-picture, becomes supreme. Nothing can shake it. You never feel that it is necessary to take anything from anybody else. You have learned that asking and seeking have, as their correlatives, receiving and finding. You know that all you have to do is to start the plastic substance of the universe flowing into the thought-moulds your picture-desire provides."

So, here's something to think about as we close this chapter. This citation of Genevieve Behrend's was written in 1921,

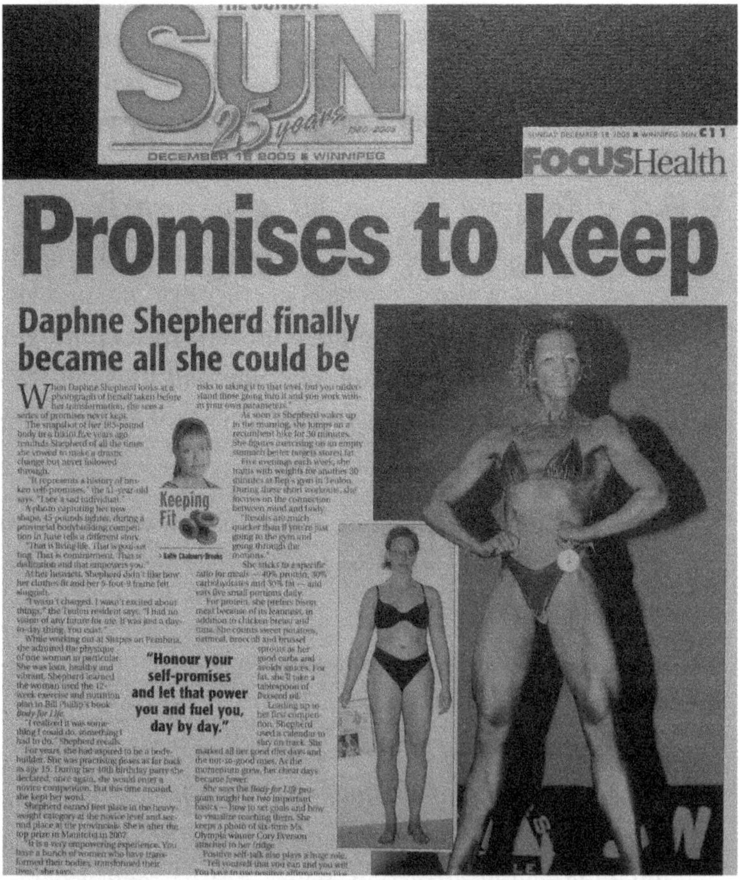

SUN 25 years 1980-2005

DECEMBER 18 2005 ■ WINNIPEG

FOCUS Health

Promises to keep

Daphne Shepherd finally became all she could be

Keeping Fit

"Honour your self-promises and let that power you and fuel you, day by day."

Figure 4 *Credit: Sun Media Corporation. Sun Media Corporation is not responsible for any claims that may be made relating to this a*rticle.

which is significant because this fundamental message has been known and implemented for centuries. For this reason, I encourage you to begin your study on yourself, energy and the laws governing our universe. If you just take the first step of action in an endeavour to learn more and understand these teachings, you create the spark that ignites the fire. As your gateways begin to open, your experience of your world will drastically shift. It is truly a fascinating and intriguing journey. The journey, your journey, is here now.

Set your intention today. Is it a bigger bank account you want? More meaningful relationships? Vacation home in a tropical setting? A fit, healthy body? Why procrastinate another moment, another day, another year? Affirm and celebrate your desire by casting your image. Then integrate and connect to it with every fibre of your being and every brain cell. See from the place that you are already in possession of it. Herein lies the power. It's your time.

Activating your Brilliance—Points to Ponder

1) The image you cast on the screen of your mind accompanied by the alignment to that desire can produce extraordinary results in every aspect of your life.

2) To eliminate or disrupt our habitual defaults, we have to decide consciously and take the necessary action to scratch the surface of the record to interrupt the grooves, so they cannot be replayed. It is then that we can consciously create and introduce new thoughts, new behaviours and entrench (habitualize) new grooves on our subconscious mind that play a different tune.

3) When it comes time for you to manifest your dream into reality, and your desire to do so is insistent, you are in exactly the right place and need to act. Recognize the insistency as one of life's pokes and move; take the first step. The universe likes speed.

~ᴏ Chapter Seven ᴏ~

From Ordinary to Extraordinary by Adding a Little "Extra"

"The will to win, the desire to succeed, the urge to reach your full potential . . . these are the keys that will unlock the door to personal excellence." —*Confucius*

The phone was on its third ring early one morning in June, 2006, and I was scrambling to find the cordless handset. I found it and answered. It was my best friend. She wanted to drop by to watch a movie she felt confident I would enjoy.

When she arrived, we caught up on all the latest and then closed the blinds in the living room to reduce the glare on the TV. As I popped the DVD in the player, I turned and asked her what it was all about. She replied that it was a movie called *The Secret,* and that it was growing wildly in popularity; like a movement of some sort. Well, that was the morning after watching the movie, that pivotal point when my life forever changed. A significant internal shift occurred.

A few months later, in August 2006, I started working earning $10.10 per hour for the local newspaper typing classified ads. I knew this was not the million dollar job I wanted to attract into my life after watching the movie The Secret in June. However, it did provide set hours, which gave me the opportunity to begin my research and studies on the law of attraction. The movie was my introduction to the law of attraction, and it made an impactful, lasting impression. In it was the promise of earning any amount of money I desired, if that is what I chose. And the promise to have, be and do anything if that is what I so desired. I was earning a bi-weekly fixed paycheque written by the company in lieu of the hours I worked for them. Oh yeah, *sure*, I wanted to earn a million dollars, have a killer physique and a convertible style Benz as my summer car in my driveway. But how?

Well, fast forward to February 2013, when I received an award from the RE/MAX organization in Las Vegas in recognition of earning over $1 million dollars in paid gross commissions at the conclusion of 2012. Along with this recognition, I had been placed in their Hall of Fame category. What has been most rewarding, has been the opportunity to pay forward and donate thousands to the Childrens Miracle Network since starting with the RE/MAX organization.

In 2011 and every year since I have also been acknowledged by our local Real Estate Board with a prestigious medallion

award that celebrates the achievements of their most successful REALTORS®.

I'm not telling you this to impress you but rather to impress
upon you that once you have resurrected your desire(s) and
a heartfelt passion to pursue that which you wish to see manifest in your life, it is all possible and waiting for you. Rest
assured that the life you are seeking is also seeking you. Is
there work involved? Absolutely there is, which is why it is
so important that you ground yourself in your truth and are
connected to your purpose. With this alignment, there will
be no resistance. Not sure of the next step? I wasn't either, but
what I do know is that when I stopped searching for my de-
finitive solution to earn, be and have, and instead tuned my
vibrational frequency in alignment with what I wanted, the
solutions presented themselves. They always will. This is the
experience with the law of attraction. It's your time.

It is paramount that I tell you these details because I was void
of any university training, only receiving a grade 12 education. I had no sales experience, although I had some Continu-
ing Ed classes at the University of Winnipeg where I received
certificates in Management Studies and Human Resource
Management. Still, I had no formal degrees, so what was it?

Success leaves clues, and in The Secret there were quotes
from Dr. Martin Luther King, Jr., Albert Einstein, Napoleon
Hill, Henry Ford and teachings of the laws that govern our
universe from such historical figures as Plato, Shakespeare,
Hugo, Newton, Emerson, Beethoven, Edison and Lincoln. In
today's world, people who also study these laws and guide us
with their wisdom are Bob Proctor, Dr. John Demartini, Dr.

Joe Vitale, Dr. Denis Waitley, Quantum Physicist Dr. John Hagelin, Lisa Nicols, Jack Canfield, John Assaraf, the late Dr. Wayne Dyer, Deepak Chopra, Esther Hayes, Dr. Michael Beckwith and many more.

So yes, that morning while sitting on the couch, watching the movie had a profound and lingering impact on me, and two things came to mind:

#1 How can all these people be wrong? We are talking not about a surface, trendy process of thought but rather the root of powerful, unadulterated thinking.

#2 I was going to meet Bob Proctor from the movie *The Secret* one day.

Along your journey as you immerse yourself in study and greater awareness, you will see there are no accidents. That is, everything happens for a reason. My personal experience watching the movie that morning accompanied by the background music and my introduction to Bob Proctor for the first time was meant to happen in my life; it was my time. The very fact that you are reading this book shows that it is meant to be. You have attracted this into your life for a reason. In *The Secret—Summary*, available as an extra on the DVD, Bob provides a synopsis that helps make sense of it all. Within the first five minutes of this summary, he asked, "What do you really want?" It was right then, that I made my decision.

That early morning in June I sat, my holster filled with a desire to succeed. I knew if I was successful at something that I was connected to and passionate about, this would lead to prosperity in all areas of my life. And so, armed with my new way of thinking and a thirst for further knowledge in its most infant stage yet filled with uncertainty, my ironclad desire and the odds stacked against me, off I went. Along the way, I reflected back to the Body-for-Life Challenge and body-building success and drew inner strength from those experiences. When you stop to think where you can draw strength, you won't have to look very far back in your life. Think of the time when you had your game face on and accomplished that goal you pursued. People say, "Oh, but Daph, that's just you." No, that's not just me. We are the extension of our Creator, Source Energy, and we ALL have these reservoirs of potential. You are an infinite self and this intelligence, this energy is in every thing and every one of us. We need to cleanse the doors of our perception and tune into the perfection that lies within. I knew that once I made the decision and committed to the process, it would come to be. Write out your previous experience from which you will draw strength in this journey ahead. Call to mind and relive your experience; reminisce and once again bask in the feeling. You did it! YOU did.

Who looks outside, dreams; Who looks inside, awakens. —*Carl Gustav Jung*

My first goal was to secure a better paying job than my job at the newspaper. I thought about all my options and there was one that came to my mind. There was a time a few years prior that I had thought of a career in real estate and actual-ly' enrolled to take the course, but at that time I came to the conclusion that it was not the right industry for me so I didn't give it any further thought. I was really just content and in my comfort zone working with the local newspaper in the classified ads department. I worked with a group of amazing individuals who were passionate about communicating local stories and the promotion of the surrounding communities, each with their unique and distinctive rural events, such as rodeos, agricultural fairs, and heartfelt stories of local people making a difference. Every day was dynamic with different content. And every department was on the move to accomplish one mission: to get the weekly paper published and distributed on time. The planning, writing, sourcing and working with advertisers, attending events, photography, layout, editing and print, then wiping the slate clean, sending out the receivables and on to inputting the next edition. It was a thrilling environment. And talk about the epitome of teamwork! I felt privileged to be a part of this unique culture.

In November 2006, it was no accident that of the three of us typing classified ads, one particular ad found its way into my basket. It was an employment ad for an office manager at RE/MAX professionals, a real estate office in Winnipeg. I quickly penned my application and was successful in securing an interview. The interview went well, though I was very nervous. When I left, I didn't have a grasp on whether the interview was a success, but I knew I gave it my all. Well, much to my surprise, a few days later I was called back for a second interview with their board of management. Once again I poured passion into my expression, but a day later learned that I didn't get the job or the $80,000/year salary it promised.

What I did walk away with, though, was a comment from Stan Newman, Broker/Owner of RE/MAX professionals that changed my life! It was a personal compliment, and he said that out of 28 applicants, I had been their second choice! Stan also went on to say that he saw great potential within me as an agent. During our conversation on the phone that day, I promised Stan that I would reinstate and finish my real estate course. And, once that was completed, I would begin a new career as a real estate agent in his office. I want to pause and point out to you here that it was Stan who recognized the inkling of talent and promise within me. I certainly didn't feel it. As a matter of fact, remember earlier that I had picked up the books but within a very short period concluded that it was not for me? The lesson is that there will be times in your life when there is an unexpected gift—a seed given to you. And as we reap, so shall we sow. Therefore, the cycle repeats itself when you pay-the-comment-forward to that person you see and acknowledge has a special gift. It is these moments when we declare our gratitude as abundance is everywhere. It is important that you as best as possible maintain an open mind to receiving, and that you are a vibrational match so that the seed takes root. It is about awareness.

"The law of divine compensation posits that this is a self-organizing and self-correcting Universe: the embryo becomes a baby, the bud becomes a blossom, the acorn becomes an oak tree. Clearly, there is some invisible force that is moving every aspect of reality to its next best expression."
—*Marianne Williamson from her book The Law of Divine Compensation: On Work, Money & Miracles*

Now, most people who interview for real estate agent positions interview once. Consumed with fear and uncertainty that was clouding my ambition, I had to interview three times: I was that unsure of myself. Let's think about this for a moment: I was earning just over $10/hour while I was going through these interviews. And yes, I could not digest the reality of the extraordinary expenses I would be incurring as a new agent from advertising to association dues coupled with the daily business expenses. With Dennis's salary, and our mortgage and car payments, it did not appear feasible to start this new career.

The last of my three interviews was with their "new agent coach," who said two things to me that took root. First, she reminded me that as children we don't know how to swim, and we will never learn if we don't take that first leap of faith into the pool. She said that yes, some of us will pop to the surface and immediately and naturally learn to tread water to stay afloat. Others will sink, take water on, sputter and struggle to keep their heads above water. But because their existence depends on the breath of air, they will persist and figure out a way to keep their heads above water.

You know, sometimes the more we struggle, the worse it gets. Why? Because as you endure, fatigue sets in. Then the fear and anxiety of "What if?" rings through you. If it is left to run rampant, it will accumulate to such a point that it spoils the whole meaning. If this has happened, or is happening, this is your signal for reflection. Sure, there are growing pains with anything new in life; however, it should not feel like an uncomfortable resistance. If you feel the threat of resistance looming, step back and assess your vibrational tone with respect to the alignment of what you want, and seek to find out why you are not feeling harmonized. Take the necessary time and dig. You are worth it, and the truth will bring such clarity to you! Trust the process; you are exactly where you are meant to be.

The second thing she enlightened me with was her comment, "Big money in, big money out." Of course, silly me! My perception and conditioning led me to base the projected real estate expenses and my ability to pay them on my *current* situation that was $10.10/hour. Kind of like when my posing suit arrived in the sandwich bag, and I temporarily backed out of competing.

Let's not let our current situations define who we are capable of becoming. The confines of this type of thinking exist only in our minds. It's a choice: stay commonplace, or make the decision to grasp the vine of life when it swings your way, and trust that you are on to something magnificent! I know there is a fountain of greatness within you. Understand that if you are not creating, you are disintegrating.

Nine months after watching the movie The Secret, I was still working for the newspaper. One morning in March 2007, my wire basket was already full of classified ads when I arrived at 8:00 that morning. These had to get done quickly because I knew that the pile was only going to get bigger as the day went on. It was just after my morning coffee break that I could finally see some progress with a dwindling pile. But this satisfaction wouldn't last for long. The mail for that day hadn't been opened or distributed yet.

The next ad on the top of the pile would be yet another life-changing moment for me. It was one of life's gentle nudges, and I immediately felt the heart tug.

It was a memorial that had been submitted by an elderly woman for her late husband who had passed one year earlier. Her handwriting was frail, large and showed evidence of a fine tremor. Her notice read:

Sir,

Please publish this memorial verse Friday, March 30.

In loving memory of Gabriel, who passed away March 21, 2006.

He walks with me down quiet paths.

We speak in wind and rain

For the magic power of memory,

Brings him back to me again.

Love as always,

Mary

I was immediately overwhelmed by emotion. I sat there absorbing each one of her beautiful letters that she sculpted with such a deep and intense love for her companion. Gabriel was no longer in her physical presence, but he was very much alive in her memory. I felt her emotion that day, and I have never forgotten. Mary's beautiful tribute validated to me there will be *that* time. It's inevitable.

Your life is precious for those you love as is their love of you. Honour yourself and the truth that lies within. Remember the infinite possibilities that are born of faith in yourself and others. Never forget. Give and always be your very best. Share your passion, and the magnificent legacy you are will leave an indelible imprint of the magic in the life you shared with them.

Life is like a promissory note, loaned to us for a while, and only paid in full when we have lived the abundant life we were meant to live. Life is not about preserving and tip-toeing, arriving safely to the grave. It's about using all our creative faculties in making a difference. It's about falling down and getting back up again. It's about being derailed and navigating through the challenges thrown our way, growing in each experience, and making your mark, thus leaving a legacy people aspire to. Our "expiry date," nobody knows. But, what I do know for sure is that your "best before" date is today, in this beautiful moment. It's your time!

Well, I knew it was my time, and I submitted my notice to the newspaper company, with my last day of work being August 10th, 2007.

On September 25th, a mere 45 days later, I had already earned $7,800.00, which was almost half my annual gross pay at the newspaper that I had been terrified to leave six weeks earlier. In 2008 I earned $94,000 and my first award with the RE/MAX organization. June 2009, I completed my broker education. In August 2009, I became a broker and was hired by Stan Newman as the training and education director for all new sales associates in his office of 105 agents. I was soon promoted to assistant manager at the RE/MAX professionals office. By early 2010, my career had sky rocketed. But balancing my increasing client list with my position at RE/MAX professionals and the two-hour commute left me exhausted. I concluded that I was playing on thin ice and made a decision to purchase a RE/MAX franchise for the Teulon market, which was approved in April 2010. In July 2010, RE/MAX Encore Realty opened in Teulon.

What I've learned through all this is that our corresponding universe likes speed and will kindly reward you when you act, when you trust and when you follow your heart. I continue to be an award-winning realtor, and with a deep sense of gratitude, I volunteer my time to mentor a Peak Producer training program in Stan's office to pay forward to him the acknowledgement and belief he had in me.

With the same precision that our laws govern the universe, the piéce de résistance in my journey was on October 19th, 2013, when I boarded a plane to Toronto to personally meet Bob Proctor. I had an unrelenting desire and personal goal to meet Bob after watching the movie The Secret in 2006. I knew with unwavering faith that it would happen as soon as I embarked upon my studies and gained a deeper understanding of the law of attraction. I just didn't know how at the time, but I trusted. Jackson Brown said, "Sometimes the heart sees what is invisible to the eye."

When the series of events took place, I was working for the newspaper—this was followed by the financial abundance through my success as a realtor—and it was clear that the universe reacted exactly the way it is supposed to. Precisely, it corresponded and aligned to manifest this event in my life. The Proctor/Gallagher Institute was holding a week long Matrixx event in Toronto that focused on personal growth in all areas of life with Bob Proctor and Sandy Gallagher. I attended this event, which has had a significant impact in every aspect of my life building upon my previous experiences. A few months following the Matrixx event, I boarded another plane to meet with Bob Proctor in Los Angeles in a more intimate setting with a handful of like-minded people. My studies continue alongside Bob who is widely regarded as one of the living masters and teachers of the Law of Attraction and Human Mind Potential and I am a teacher and consultant of the Proctor Gallagher *Thinking into Results* program.

What I once considered to be outrageous and unlikely due to once-present circumstance had completely manifested in my life and continues to bloom as I continue to nurture, build on positive thoughts and practise the ever-unfolding dynamics of the law of attraction in my life.

Today is the first day of the rest of your life. It's your time!

Ask yourself, "What do I really want?" Maybe you want to make a difference in the lives of others. How? Be a visionary, live a life of co-creative design and dream big. Make your list, and write it down in the present tense. As you are writing, feel the flood of emotion knowing that you are already living and in possession of what you want. Come *from* that place. Remember, this is where the shift occurs, and you emit a vibrational frequency that corresponds to the universe's song. Trust and know that it will come to be.

How is your life or your present circumstance? Are there any aspects of it that you would like to expand upon? What have you to lose by reading up a little and further exploring the law of attraction? Think of a towrope at the bottom of a ski hill. To get to the top of the hill, you grab a hold, and in a short while you are there. As you rise higher, you are exposed to breathless views and the stunning undertakings of Mother Nature. Commit to holding on in your quest, as you will see that the view from the top will be nothing short of "sun" sational! You will also gain an incredible amount of insight and wisdom along the way.

Activating your Brilliance—Points to Ponder

1) When you are in vibrational alignment with your truth, what you desire will come to manifest for you with little resistance.

2) The lesson is that there will be times in your life when there is an unexpected gift, like a seed given to you. And as we reap, so shall we sow. Therefore, the cycle repeats itself when you pay-the-comment-forward to that person you see and acknowledge has a special gift. Make a point today to pay forward a compliment. Work toward a daily ritual of always leaving someone with the impression of increase.

3) If you feel the threat of resistance looming, step back and assess your vibrational tone with respect to the alignment of what you want and seek to find out why you are not feeling harmonized. Take the necessary time, and dig because you are worth it, and the truth will bring such clarity to you! Journal this journey.

Chapter Eight

The Must-Have Emotion

The law of attraction states that within our universe, nothing is at rest. Everything is moving at a high rate of vibration, and everything we need, all the resources, is right here, right now. As we increase our level of awareness, we align with our truth and harmonize our vibrational frequency. We are vibrational beings, existing in a vibrational universe. We are electrically charged beings, and we live in an ocean of motion.

Let's think back to our high school Chemistry 101 class for a moment. At the base level, we are made of atoms, and within the atoms are polar opposite electrical charges. Moving rapidly around the nucleus of the atom are electrons. Atoms join up and make molecules. Molecules make up organelles, the small organs in each cell. The cells then are the building blocks of life, wrapped with membranes.

Great! Is it all coming back to you? Okay, stay with me just a bit longer. Our tissues are made of cells that work in unison to perform various functions. These tissues make up our organs. There are eleven major organ systems within us: integumentary, skeletal, muscular, circulatory, nervous, respiratory, digestive, urinary, endocrine, reproductive and lymphatic or immune. The sum of these organ systems is an organism, like a person or an animal. All organisms on this planet use vibration or energy as the primary means of communication, and every atom and every molecule absorbs and radiates energy, including you. We are, therefore, radiating energy or creating "vibes" that are our unique signature. Have you ever been in the presence of someone who you intuitively felt had a bad "vibe"? Think about that for a moment. How does this happen when you haven't even exchanged a word? Well, this is your intuitive feedback that the person was not a vibrational match and was in contrast to your "vibe".

So you see we are electrically charged beings, vibrating at a high frequency, and have enormous amounts of ever-present electric potential within us. Our nerve impulses are the electricity in the body, and neurons are the basic unit of the nervous system. Neurons are responsible for sending, receiving and interpreting information from all parts of the body. The human nervous system can create electric energy waves that can be measured with scientific instruments. Case in point: the ECG machine that measures the electrical impulses of the heart. Our thoughts also have a frequency and can also be measured. Each thought vibrates at a certain frequency. Fascinating, isn't it?

We can create and control what we think about in our reasoning mind, the conscious mind. And, it's our choice to accept or reject those thoughts. That's our entitlement, our privilege. And so it follows that if we can create and control our thoughts, then those thoughts can influence us and those around us. We create our reality through thought. With our thoughts, we can sift through, choose and appreciate the tremendous variety of contrast offered that is ours to consider and conclude from.

Let's delve a little deeper. Deep within each of us are natural impulses, desires, conclusions, decisions, truths, thoughts, determinations and intentions. These are formulated by what we focus on and then implemented or created through us. Focus is said to be your deliberate creation of that which you desire. The moment you decide, collective consciousness is summoned, and the resources you require for the unfoldment of your reality will appear. What you are thinking, considering or focused on, and that which you are in receipt of, will always be a direct vibrational match.

Therefore, it is critical that you audit and observe what is currently in your life. What is working and what is not? Understand that if you are not vibrating in harmony with that which you desire, it cannot come to manifest for you. You must be aligned, an exact vibrational match to what it is that you are feeling and thinking.

Our must-have emotion, then, is your "feeling" emotion, as this will tell you what frequency or vibration you are emitting, and whether it is good or bad. Much like the thermostat in your home, we set them to a comfortable temperature conducive to a nice relaxing experience at home. The kids come in, the dog goes out, and over a short period the temperature slowly begins to drop as the warm air escapes the home. Our thermostat senses the deviation from the original preset temperature to the current ambient room temperature. There is a discrepancy. It then sends a signal to activate the furnace, so the original preset temperature can be restored.

So, how does that relate to us in our everyday living? Well, your emotions are a remarkable, built-in indicator that tells us when our temperature is off. Earlier, I said that it is important that you feel good. In our example, let's establish the emotion of "feeling good" as your base "comfort" temperature. And so, when we feel good, we are generally taking things in stride and overall enjoying life. But then along comes an aggravation. And what happens next? We respond adversely adopting a negative emotion: we're annoyed. Simultaneously, your thermostat/indicator senses this deviation from the base preset, and the emotional drop in temperature summons us that we're off course.

In order to get back on track, we will require a good-feeling emotion to come along and reinstate our comfortable ambient temperature preset once again. How do we do that? Simple: we need positive stimulus. What does that look like? Well, what makes you feel good? For me, it's listening to music, exercising, enjoying a ride on my Harley or a lazy afternoon at home with my cat and a good book in hand with my special "gratitude" smoothie. The thoughts that bring about good feelings mean you are on the right track. The thoughts that bring about bad feelings means you are not on the right track, and remember: whatever it is that you are feeling is a perfect reflection of what is in the process of becoming.

Let's take a quick look back at the law of attraction, which decrees that like attracts like. That is, you attract into your life whatever you focus on. Therefore, positive thoughts attract positive events. Negative thoughts will attract negative events. All this is processed through you and your thoughts, and the vibrational frequency you establish and emit creates your current reality. Do you see how now and why it is critical that you feel good? If you neglect to pay attention to how you are feeling, you end up with no basis of knowing which direction to go because you have not established an emotional base (preset) from which to draw contrast.

It is neither my intention nor the intention of this book to complicate all the "reasons" behind our emotions. It's much simpler than that. There are two categories: positive feel-good emotions and negative or bad emotions.

Positive feedback emotions	Negative feedback emotions
Happy	Unhappy
Loving	Resentful
Thankful	Fearful
Passionate	Worry
Joyful	Doubtful
Excited	Angry
Hopeful	Critical
Satisfied	Anxiety
Grateful	

So, if you want to harness the creative power to bring more of the good things in your life, start to make feeling good a priority. Nothing is more important than you coming from the place of feeling good.

As you begin to feel better, you will know that you are aligned with that which you desire to make manifest in your life. Incrementally, you shift your current reality with new-formed conclusions that are your springboard to the next level.

"Nature abhors a vacuum." —*Aristotle*

As you allow yourself to feel good, and your thoughts are aligned in this vibration, you begin to release and replace the negative emotions. By releasing the negative influences in your life, that void will be filled with positive influences. As this happens, the inner conversation changes and transitions to one that supports, serves and nurtures you on your journey. You are a powerful, conscious creator, and by observing the content and canvas of your current reality and the manifestations in your life, you are better able to assess what vibration you have been broadcasting. And when your emotions intersect, you can achieve a positive state more easily and revert to your desired temperature.

What vibration are you offering? What are you thinking and feeling right now? Look at the results around you. Many times throughout your life, you have to audit and take self-stock. If it is not what you want and your life is just not working in your favour, then it is time to reset the thermostat. Accept this as an on-going privilege in the quest to a life deliberately created by you and on your terms.

A most empowering consideration is that you can begin right where you are, right now. It is instantaneous gratification; no credit cards required, and it is what you can do today. Affirm and honour yourself by declaring, "I will do that today." Nothing matters but this very moment. The point of power is this very moment and what you are focusing your attention on. It is just as simple as making a choice to take that first step. It's your time!

Activating your Brilliance—Points to Ponder

1) We are radiating energy or creating "vibes" that are our unique signature. Be cognizant of your emotions and vibrational tone today and journal your experiences. Do this diligently for the next thirty days and compare your experiences.

2) What you are thinking, considering or focused on, and that which you are in receipt of, will always be a direct vibrational match. You are always with yourself. Every thought, every action belongs to you. If you are seeking abundance and fulfilment you must realize that it is only within yourself that you will find them. Furnish your inner dwelling with joy, love and gratitude and it will be the place that you never want to leave. You will have established pure contentment within.

3) Our must-have emotion is your *feeling* emotion, as this will tell you what frequency or vibration you are emitting, good or bad. Nothing is more important than that you come from the place of feeling good. This will be accomplished when you stand in the essence of who you are.

Chapter Nine

A Stifled Life Behind Bars

*V*isualize a sterile, untapped landscape of mental clarity: a clean slate from which you can begin to plant the seeds of your desires with the creative potential that lies within you. If you are resisting, or apprehensive, or you think to yourself, "I'll do that later," then that's the acknowledgement of where you are currently. It is also confirmation and direct feedback that there is work for you to do. These are the starting blocks of a challenge though, that you're going to love!

Ask yourself what is holding you back. What is stopping you from reaping great prosperity and productivity? Are you comfortable with where you are on your life path and with what you have as a reflection of that? Are you content? Complacency may be okay for some, but the fact that you're reading this book and have gotten this far in it indicates there is much more for you. Being comfortable is stalemate, a deadlock; a situation in which little or no progress can be made or where advancement is impossible. Indecisiveness, procrastination and the "should I's?" can also result in stagnation. This is not in harmony with the creative process. We are here to create and to express life in all its awesome beauty. Spirit is always for expression and fuller expansion and this will always be. Creation is the rhythm and cycle in life as in all of nature. You either create or disintegrate. The creative, always-present, potential energy is ours. Choose to live magnificently. It's your time!

The problem and setback for many of us stems way back to our childhood. As infants, we lacked the ability to make conscious decisions, as we had no basis or contrast. All habits and patterns were passed along to us by our parents, our environment or caregivers and were impressed upon our subconscious minds. We behaved much like our parents, and we were genetically influenced by many of their attributes, including stature, and physical appearances such as hair, skin tone, facial features, and physiological characteristics like blood types and predisposition to systemic deficiencies, high blood pressure, diabetes, etc.

Then, it was off to school. We were taught from stacks of books. We were also taught how to write words and string them into meaningful sentences. We learned about math and numbers, about literature and history and about science and nature.

I learned to play sports. I learned about Shakespeare. I also learned about drafting, French and anthropology among a host of other subjects. But I never learned about how or *why* I thought and did things the way I did. I wasn't taught how to *really* think or how our thoughts are processed, which is the highest function we are capable of as human beings.

I was graded on what I could memorize, my ability to recall how to put concepts in chronological order and how well I was able to articulate. If I fell short, I failed. In my school years, conformity was stressed. If you were a little different, repercussions always seemed to follow. Some kids were mean, and teachers wanted you to act a particular way. Ideas were impressed upon you, with little expressed by you. Well, I didn't act the way they wanted me to. And I spent a lot of time in detention, supposedly there to think about their perspective of my "unwelcome" actions. I was a kid being a kid. Running in the parking lot puddles with my friends, having puddle parties by kicking water at each other, and then not being allowed to enter the classroom with damp pants. Oh golly, and then the punishment by writing lines: "I will not run in puddles anymore during school hours." x 250. I wasn't a really bad kid. But I did talk a lot, which also fast-tracked me to a couple more sessions of line writing: "I will not talk and disrupt the class," x 250. It's ironic that today I make a comfortable living by talking. Do you think that perhaps back then it was an early expression of my natural ability to communicate and network effectively and perhaps should have been cultivated rather than supressed?

I was a "C" student for the most part, and I earned a few "B's" and "D's" along the way. I didn't make grade 12 graduation, so I had to go to summer school. After passing the last few credits there, my grade 12 diploma was mailed to me. Now what? I had no direction, and based on my report cards, I was unlikely to go to university. If my report card was a mirror image of the life I would live beyond my school years, I was in big trouble. This "graded" life of mine was how I departed the scholastic years and stepped into my working years with low self-esteem. I certainly wasn't looking through rose-coloured glasses depicting a bright picture for my future.

My poor self-esteem was amplified by the absence of a biological makeup because I was adopted. I was grasping for clues as to what I might be good at, and I wondered what my biological parents were good at. What did they do professionally? I thought this may have helped in providing me a clue for a career direction, but it was not to be.

So, off I went and started working as a waitress at a local restaurant. My next job was as a receptionist, then as a secretary. I enjoyed the pulse of the corporate world and started to take some courses in business administration, human resources and business management.

I was travelling up the corporate ladder one rung at a time. I worked both in the private and government sectors and realized that the higher I climbed, the more office politics and adversities I experienced. As a compassionate person, I concluded that corporate Winnipeg was not the playground I wanted to play in. In reflection, I intuitively felt an on-going nagging resistance in my corporate pursuit. That intuition was the whisper from my subconscious mind prompting me that I was on the wrong path. Had I known what I know now in awareness, all the obstacles and challenges I endured and trekked through for all those years were purposely orchestrated so that I would realign to my true purpose. Have you been feeling an on-going resistance to something? If you are feeling a resistance, write it out in detailed order. How long have you been feeling this way? What do you believe is the root cause of this conflict? Is it your thoughts? Who is involved? Is there a bigger message for you? Could there be?

As my passion for corporate Winnipeg began to erode, I concluded I needed a change, so I started studies in massage therapy. For three years, and for the first time in my life, I was academically successful, which validated that I was aligned with my truth and core purpose. There was little resistance during my studies, and I thoroughly enjoyed the challenge of the academics. Once graduated, I rented space in a chiropractor's office offering massage therapy as an alternative modality for treatment for our joint patients. In 1994, my mom opened a massage therapy college in Winnipeg, and I eventually joined her and taught the business course and was registrar until her retirement. I continued working part-time in my clinic, and had a second therapist fill in on days when I was working at the college. As the college grew, more of my time was required, so I sold my clinic and worked full-time at the college.

The college atmosphere was special in that I was able to work alongside my mom, brother and sister, as well as some of the best instructors in the province in anatomy, kinesiology, sports massage and more! When the college was sold, my mom was able to live out her dream of travelling to and sculpting in Italy. It was a challenging and sad time because we all worked so well together, passionate about our work and the heart of the college, our students. And so, I went back to what I knew, back into my comfort zone, and secured an administrative job in corporate Winnipeg.

I went back to office work because it was familiar, and I was good at it. I confined myself to the "same old, same old," because I lacked the ability to recognize that I was settling for things as they were.

Many of us are living a "limited" life. The good news is we are limited only within the confines of our own minds, which means we can change this. We form habits, some passed down, others we establish, and in all this, we have the capacity and conscious ability to either accept or reject the ideas and habits we abide by; to determine if they are working for us or not. We are in control, but much of the time we conform to the masses. Because that's what everyone else is doing, and it's comfortable and familiar.

> You cannot escape a prison if you don't know you're in one. —*Bob Proctor*

Isn't it time you lovingly gave yourself permission and free rein to grow and transcend into your greatness? Isn't it time that you explored *you?* Isn't it time that you stopped being so hard on yourself for the in-harmonies that were impressed upon you, which have caused chaos and turmoil in your life because they did not resonate with your true spiritual purpose? Isn't it time that you abolish the thoughts that you are not living in accordance with everyone else's standard: society's standard based on last month's sales sheet, last quarter's report card, yesterday's transaction record or the supper you overcooked or that you were late picking the kids up from piano lessons? You see, we allow our senses to control our result which is backwards. In doing so, we are letting the outside world define us.

It's time to step off the merry-go-round and reframe our thoughts. *The only limitations in our lives are the limits we are placing on ourselves.* Repeat that sentence slowly and aloud, for this alone should generate that spark which will empower you to plant your foot assuredly for that first step to unearthing your beautiful purpose. So many of us look at our current state of affairs, our bank balances, asset sheet, cars we drive, clothes we wear, and succumb to the thought that this is what defines us: this is who we are.

No! That is ego speaking. Your current circumstances are a reflection of your conditioning, not your shrouded potential. This is where you change your self-talk, sift through and intentionally choose what you are allowing to filter into your subconscious mind, begin to alter your conditioning and declare, "No, that is who I was!" Call to mind that you are the creator of your reality and do so with your thoughts. Otherwise, you create a trap for yourself. Let your new life-fulfilling images and desires guide you and break the chains of your limiting beliefs. They have no part in any creative process. New ideas, thoughts and images liberate tremendous energy and will transform your life. It's your time!

Quit flying below the clouds. Establish a directive for yourself, a life script and remember that your life is always under construction. Endure the turbulence until the break into the azure sky awards you with warmth and unlimited possibilities. Your desires are your vessel. Dare to suspend your limiting beliefs, and you will experience sound living on your terms. When your new voice and visions become more pronounced than the outside chatter and opinions, then you are on your way to living an authentic and prosperous life as scribed by you. Trust that there can be no progress without change. If nothing changes . . . nothing changes.

Listen to the voice within. Take notice of life's gentle nudges, which come to you in the form of intuitions, hunches, impulses, urges or perhaps words spoken by a stranger. How do you differentiate these from other emotions? Their debut appearance may make you feel uneasy, awkward and even out of sync. But, stay tuned. Here's an interesting parallel I want to share with you . . . the words *listen and silent* have identical letters and are the necessary partners in muting the mind and opening the channels to receive the remedial flow of infinite intelligence. Work to identify the imbalances and contrasts in your life, and know that from these an opportunity to grow or renew lies before you. These contrasts emulate a blank canvas from which you begin to colour your life different from these.

We know that any thought or resulting belief can be contagious and gain momentum, whether it is negative or positive. Negative thoughts = negative results; positive thoughts = positive results. Choose positively, and allow the influence of those thoughts to ignite the power within. Keep your conscious mind busy bathing in expectation. That is, the expected benefit *from* already having that which you desire in your physical experience. The polar opposite will be submission to bad thoughts and circumstances, and you are defeated before you set out. Asphyxiated by your own internal dialogue.

You can, and I encourage you to, choose extraordinary living and say, "Life is proceeding through me by me, and the way I shape my thoughts and ideas will change my experience." Don't let circumstance or the outside world shape your experiences. That would be a life lived in the company of a pool of piranhas. You apply your thought to your experience; draw your conclusion and take control. You are the artisan of your life. Dare to step outside conformity.

Risk believing in yourself! Toss aside the excuses, and take the first step toward that opportunity you've been ignoring. Understand that until now, the only thing that has been standing in the way is you. It is you who have placed the limits on yourself. We weren't born with negative, fearful or limiting beliefs. These are learned characteristics. You were born from an eternal and omnipresent love that seeks to preserve your life, a life of expansion and expression. Always remember this.

Here's the thing: we call it an injustice when someone has been wrongly convicted and spends a fraction of their life imprisoned. When the jury overturns the decision of a wrongful conviction, the prisoner is significantly rewarded in lieu of precious time lost. Do you feel imprisoned in any aspect of your life? If so, it's time to overturn your ill serving decision and trust that you as well will be rewarded generously through your experiences of fulfilled living. You be the judge of you. Are you serving a life sentence, imprisoned by the confines and limiting beliefs in your own mind? Don't spend another moment behind those bars; you've already paid dearly through the lessons and experiences you have endured until now. Choose freedom—It's your time!

Activating your Brilliance—Points to Ponder

1) Creation is the rhythm and cycle in life as in all of nature. You either create or disintegrate.

2) When your new voice and visions become more pronounced than the outside chatter and opinions, then you are on your way to living an authentic and prosperous life as scribed by you.

3) We weren't born with negative, fearful or limiting beliefs. These are learned characteristics. We were born from an eternal and omnipresent love that seeks to preserve your life, a life of expansion and expression. Always remember this.

Chapter Ten

Your Radical Departure

*T*oday is a gift. Give thanks that you have been granted today to do or to be anything you desire.

Like a book, your life is an accumulation of blank pages upon which you, the author, can write your story. Think of one page being equal to one day of your life and the chapters as your life experience milestones. The cover represents your birth and should be extraordinary in colour, emotion and pizzazz, as was the day you were brought into this world. The back cover denotes the end of your physical presence and journey on earth.

What would the title of your book be? It is only from this place that you can begin to map out where you will go. You need a plan and a crystal clear vision of what you want. Feed your emotions full of the experience of already being in possession of that which you desire. Parallel to this, the key to tapping into the powerhouse of your subconscious will be the critical daily undertaking of reading your vision or gratitude statement. Let's get started. Find a piece of paper wherever you are right now. It can be a napkin, the back of someone's business card or the envelope from your mailbox this morning. Please follow through with this very important step. Imagine the fulfilment of your desire over and over again; see it, feel it, taste it, intend it and embrace it. For example:

"I am so happy and grateful now that I am working in my dream job as a home designer for which I am generously compensated through my salary of $100,000.00 and a client list that continues to grow."

Take time in this moment to write out your gratitude statement. Back in my bodybuilding days, I can see where I made a mistake. During times when I lacked direction, I drifted and lost a great deal of precious training time. It is crucial that you express your desires in your gratitude statement in a positive nature. The conversation with yourself has to change inside, enabling you to bid farewell to your past patterns of thinking and conditioning. Here are a few examples:

Old Pattern of Thinking	New Conversation with Self
"I think I can lose weight."	"I love how I look and feel, and I am so happy and grateful to have this beautiful body."
"I might be able to . . ."	"I am so happy and grateful that I am doing . . ."
"I hope to get the job promotion."	"I am so happy and grateful and absolutely love working for . . . !"

Here is yet another humbling example on the workings of the law of attraction. In 1996 I was working as an administrative assistant, and there was a magazine in the lobby area. On my lunch hour, I sat down to eat and flipped through the pages. There was an advertisement from Mercedes-Benz for their SL Class convertible with the caption, "If life were fair, we would all have one." Well, I fell in love with this car but knew I could never afford one. I was mesmerized by its beauty and secretly tore the picture out.

Building upon my experience and business success, coupled with my studies of the law of attraction, I resurrected that picture in 2008, and on the screen on my mind, I owned that car. The next step was to become emotionally involved with the car. So I went to the Mercedes-Benz dealership, and took an SLK convertible for a test drive. It was pure, fuel-injected bliss! We got out, and Dennis took my picture sitting at the wheel and standing beside the car. At the time, I had no idea how I could ever make this materialize. I etched the whole experience in my subconscious mind from the smell of the leather, the vibration of the accelerator underfoot and the warm wind whisking through my hair. I trusted the process, connected, and was very clear on what I wanted. I was immersed in gratitude being the proud owner of my dream car. That was the ever-present image and conversation with myself in August, 2008.

On September 10th, 2009, I brought Sasha home. A Mercedes-Benz SLK 350 convertible, which exceeded my wildest dreams! There is another universal law we'll touch briefly on called the law of gestation, which decrees that every seed has a gestation period. Our ideas and thoughts are our spiritual seeds.

Well, the seed had been planted in 1996 when I tore that page out of the magazine. Once I began my studies in 2007, I knew exactly what I needed to do, and 13 short months after our test drive, the car of my dreams manifested into form for me.

Figure 5 *Dream machine*

Seriously, what is it that you want to experience or have? Is it a family vacation? Is it to find a life partner? To learn a new hobby? Is it a thriving bank account you want? Is it to reconnect with an old friend? Learn to sculpt or paint? A healthy body? Are you willing to embrace the reality that anything you desire can unfold and manifest for you? It will be the greatest journey that you have ever embarked on and a radical departure from the familiarity that you have come to know.

It's your time to stretch, and let go of the resistance. Spirit desires expansion for fuller expression of self. Acknowledge that thought on every level of your being. Awaken your cells, and let this message translate to the organs and systems that make up your physical being. Defy logic when thinking of what you want. Logic is captivity . . . an intellectual prison. Understand that transformations do not happen all at once. Many small corrections take place along the way.

In our hurried and over-stimulated world, it is difficult to stop the insanity and step off the merry-go-round of life that is making our heads spin. A lot of us fail to recognize how wound up we really are. But the evidence is widespread, and you don't have to look very far to see how this is affecting us as a populace. There are increased incidents of road rage, bullying and gang violence to name just a few. There is increased substance abuse. Addictions as coping mechanisms for some who need to escape and mute their life experiences. There is the expectation of instant gratification, and when all these incidents are stirred in uncertainty, the outcome is unrest and agitation. We cannot continue this way as it is the personal path to a destructive finale that is rooted in fear, doubt and uncertainty. Fearful of not having enough; perceived limitations, fearful of what the other person is thinking, fearful that we might lose something—jobs, status, health, fearful of world events. Fearful that we are not enough. Our reaction is to put our heads down, close our doors to the outside and micromanage our lives, rarely coming up for a breath. Fear-based behaviours breed anxiety; worry and doubt and this in turn establishes that vibration.

It is time that we start to live life not trapped in fear. The great news is that we already possess the power to step beyond these perceived boundaries. There is work to do if we wish to evolve. If we continue suspended in the whirlwind of all our daily responsibilities and in micromanagement, life will elude us and we will lose time, precious time.

Be cognizant of your time here. Think about the expression "I can't believe how time flies."

If time were dollar bills, you would take stock of your cash pile on a regular basis. If it was quickly diminishing you would be alarmed and rapidly get a handle on where the dollar bills were going, because if you didn't, there would be no way to pay the mortgage, no way to feed the kids, no way to pay the bills, no way to buy clothes or provide necessities. Think of time as your personal currency. Become acutely aware of where you are spending it and whether your return on investment, your ROI, brings you fulfillment. Invest wisely.

Life's moments are priceless. Make frequent deposits in your emotional bank account, nourish and sustain it, and you will be amazed at your inner personal wealth. Keep mindlessly spending it, though, and you may experience an intellectual bankruptcy that quickly qualifies you for membership into the "I wish I would have" club.

Reconnect with your inner child and resuscitate that wonderful intellectual gift inside yourself called *imagination*. You know, I had no idea how to sculpt a better body or how to earn in excess of a million dollars in a relatively short period, in a profession I knew nothing about, or that I would be driving my dream car today. I did begin, though, to understand where I was currently and that the desire to achieve great things was about an awareness in harmonizing and honouring my spiritual DNA. It requires no modification or improvements; it is all-knowing, it is all-powerful, and it is ever-present always and everywhere.

As I took stock of where I was, I knew there had to be a shift in thinking—a radical departure from the old way—and that my desires and commitments needed to speak louder than my fears. It was my time, and I had to trust the process and start, whether I was ready or not. Disintegrating was not an option for me, nor should it be for you. You're either going forward or going backward. Nothing stands still, and status quo is a fast track to intellectual and spiritual demise.

"All the breaks you need in life wait within your imagination. Imagination is the workshop of your mind, capable of turning mind energy into accomplishment and wealth." —*Napoleon Hill*

Remember, it's your book, based on your life experiences, and nobody else can write that for you. Begin today to write on your first blank page with colour, with love and enthusiasm, unlike you've ever felt before, and trust that what you've written will plant the seed for it to manifest and bloom before you.

Activating your Brilliance—Points to Ponder

1) Like a book, your life is an accumulation of blank pages upon which you, the author, can write your story.

2) Understand that transformations do not happen all at once. Many small corrections take place along the way.

3) Life's moments are priceless. Make frequent deposits in your emotional bank account, nourish and sustain it, and you will be amazed at your inner personal wealth.

Chapter Eleven

It's Your Time...
What Comes Next?

egin by feeling good today. Know that you are in great company. Many others have already pioneered the trail that you seek before you. Embrace a heightened level of awareness with a light and loving heart. Understand how the laws of the universe work and what your part and responsibility are within this framework. Look around you and understand that everything that now exists was once imagined from the same creative faculties that lie within you.

We must make a choice to step forward and trust and commit to the process with relentless confidence and faith. Write out a directive to yourself. What do you want with the time remaining in your life? Transcribe a life of design, of deliberate creation. This is the greatest gift you can give to yourself. It is your pure truth and the essence of who you are.

Memories of good times are to be cherished. Find time to celebrate them. Memories of turbulent times are teachers. Prolonged thinking or dwelling on turbulent times past, though, is a waste, as it will only make certain that the future will be a direct reflection of the past. Remember, you become what you think about most of the time.

Acknowledge that if you are not stepping forward in growth, you are stepping back into safety. Let's not go to the grave with the music still in us, in a good-looking and well-preserved body. Rather, let's arrive tuckered out, thoroughly spent and outta gas proclaiming, "Holy crap! What a trip!" Our bodies are our "ride" while on planet earth. We are not physical beings having a spiritual experience rather we are spiritual beings having a physical experience.

Do not worry what others are thinking. You control you, and you are living life on your terms. Put your energy into your goals, not in defending who or where you are. You have an internal compass, follow it and stop hindering your progress. If we can let go and allow we will be guided to living a life on purpose. This takes practise.

> "And those who were seen dancing were thought to be insane by those who could not hear the music." —*Friedrich Nietzsche*

What is it you desire? Think big. Do not worry how or when it is going to happen. Sow the seeds, and the universe will respond. Dream with no limits. You must believe that abundance is your birthright. Come from the place as though you already possess these great things. Please don't ever give up on your dreams due to the amount of time you think it may take to achieve them for the time will pass anyway.

Write out your goals and desires on a card. Carry this card with you at all times and read it, and become inspired by it several times a day. In present tense, write and rehearse, "I am so happy and grateful now that I am . . . (fill in the blank)."

Journal your experiences and frequently express gratitude for the magnificent life you are living. Print out calendars, as I did when bodybuilding and map out your journey, for this will be the first of many wonderful journeys to come. To do this accurately, you have to know where you are. This is where you spend quiet time in reflection. Evaluate what is in harmony with you and what it is that you feel is depleting your core spiritual being.

Exercise is important, and our bodies are built to move. There are a wide variety of ways to accomplish this, but the key element is that you move. Your body as mentioned previously, is a miraculous organism and is your "ride" or "vehicle" for your soul to have an experience here in this world. It is a gift to you. I have found that exercise helps me in two ways. First, it fuels my energy reservoir so that I am more than capable of fulfilling my daily tasks with unmatched zest and enthusiasm. Second, exercise has been effective from a healing standpoint. During my workouts, and in my mind, my sweat impersonates tears. The first 10 minutes of my sweat, I allow my body to cry for all the injustices I have come to know personally or within our global community. My final 20 minutes are when I sweat tears of joy. Happy tears that

I am honouring, loving and nourishing my spirit and body temple for which I am so very grateful.

Practice being still. Embrace lingering moments in which you feel good and connected to your truth. With your hand on your diaphragm, take a deep breath and relax your shoulders. Enhance your experience further by integrating soothing music or sounds of nature. Utilize these peaceful moments as an opportunity to open your heart to allow light to illuminate your path to your core truths. Be still and allow yourself to be lived by it and trust that you will be guided. Express all that you are grateful for. Now, listen.

Trust the process and have faith. Eliminate the paralyzing confines of fear. When we worry and doubt, fear is born within us. This sets up a negative vibration, which is expressed as anxiety through the body. Start to rid the worry and doubt by studying the laws by which we are governed, and this will eliminate the ignorance in which worry and doubt are incubated.

Treat others as you would want to be treated, keeping in mind that we are one. Learn to respect others, and understand that they, too, have been conditioned by their environments. Do not judge. Let go of your expectation of others and this will avoid disappointments in your own life. Learn from the differences, as they will draw contrast for you in your life, which you can choose to embrace or let be. Always leave others with the feeling of increase. We all share in this infinite universe and what we really need to embrace is love . . . its the only way to survive. Individuality is an illusion borne from ego.

You are a beautiful human being of infinite possibilities, capable of creating an outstanding and marvellous life with your time remaining. Be generous and make every moment count!

These I know for sure.

Do you know what else I know for sure? It's your time! Enjoy this magnificent journey called your life, and I look forward to our paths crossing and to connecting with you along the way.

Namasté, Brightlight!

Daphne

"Let us not look back in anger, nor forward in fear, but around us in awareness."
—*James Thurber*

For More Information: Look within yourself.

About the Author

*D*aphne Shepherd is an expert in results. She is a successful real estate broker and owner of RE/MAX Encore Realty. Daphne has received the highest accolades for her award-winning service both within the RE/MAX organization and her local real estate board. She is an accomplished bodybuilder and has a beautiful holistic aura as a result of extensive training and years of experience as a massage therapist.

Growing up, she was recognized with the prestigious *Order of Sport Excellence* award from the Province of Manitoba for her skills in volleyball and in 2001 was a Top Finisher in the Body-for-Life Challenge, placing in the top 0.30% of 700,000 applicants worldwide. Her dedication has blazed a magnificent life path, which has brought her phenomenal success in all aspects of her life including health, spiritual wealth, happiness and financial abundance.

Daphne is a *Thinking into Results* Consultant that has immersed herself in a lifelong study of the power of thoughts alongside Bob Proctor who is widely regarded as one of the living masters and teachers of the Law of Attraction and Human Mind Potential. Daphne is a student of Napoleons Hills masterpiece "'Think and Grow Rich" which in turn has inspired reading from a whole genre of success philosophy books.

Daphne is all about getting it done. If you're at a crossroad in life and feeling an internal stir that is telling you that it's your time, Daphne has the "know how" to close the gap in getting you exactly what you want. She is an inspirational role model that has walked the walk and offers corporate training, seminars and one-on-one consulting.

Daphne resides in a small community with her husband, Dennis. Their recreation time is spent riding their Harleys, travelling, or nestled together with their outrageous cat, Mr. Benjamin.

www.ingramcontent.com/pod-product-compliance
Lightning Source LLC
Chambersburg PA
CBHW072019040426
42447CB00009B/1665